The History of South Africa

CRAFTED BY SKRIUWER

Copyright © 2025 by Skriuwer.

All rights reserved. No part of this book may be used or reproduced in any form whatsoever without written permission except in the case of brief quotations in critical articles or reviews.

At **Skriuwer**, we're more than just a team—we're a global community of people who love books. In Frisian, "Skriuwer" means "writer," and that's at the heart of what we do: creating and sharing books with readers worldwide. Wherever you are in the world, **Skriuwer** is here to inspire learning.

Frisian is one of the oldest languages in Europe, closely related to English and Dutch, and is spoken by about **500,000 people** in the province of **Friesland** (Fryslân), located in the northern Netherlands. It's the second official language of the Netherlands, but like many minority languages, Frisian faces the challenge of survival in a modern, globalized world.

We're using the money we earn to promote the Frisian language.

For more information, contact : **kontakt@skriuwer.com** (www.skriuwer.com)

Disclaimer:
The images in this book are creative reinterpretations of historical scenes. While every effort was made to accurately capture the essence of the periods depicted, some illustrations may include artistic embellishments or approximations. They are intended to evoke the atmosphere and spirit of the times rather than serve as precise historical records.

TABLE OF CONTENTS

CHAPTER 1: EARLY SOUTH AFRICA AND THE FIRST PEOPLE

- Evidence of some of the oldest human tools in South Africa
- Stone Age developments and hunting-gathering societies
- Beginnings of spiritual beliefs and rock art

CHAPTER 2: THE KHOISAN AND THEIR WAY OF LIFE

- Khoikhoi herders and San hunter-gatherers
- Click-based languages and cultural traditions
- Trade, conflicts, and alliances with incoming groups

CHAPTER 3: THE BANTU MIGRATIONS AND NEW SETTLEMENTS

- Origins and spread of Bantu-speaking farmers
- Ironworking, agriculture, and social organization
- Interactions with Khoisan peoples and emerging chiefdoms

CHAPTER 4: THE GROWTH OF EARLY AFRICAN KINGDOMS

- Formation of influential states like Mapungubwe
- Trade connections, gold, and cultural centers
- Social hierarchies and religious rituals

CHAPTER 5: THE ARRIVAL OF THE PORTUGUESE EXPLORERS

- Bartolomeu Dias, Vasco da Gama, and the Cape Route
- Early encounters with coastal peoples
- Shipwrecks and the castaway stories shaping local awareness

CHAPTER 6: DUTCH SETTLEMENT AT THE CAPE

- Establishment of a refreshment station in 1652
- Jan van Riebeeck's administration and growth of farms
- Conflict with Khoisan and introduction of slavery

CHAPTER 7: BRITISH INFLUENCE AND THE CAPE COLONY

- Seizure of the Cape during European wars
- Legal reforms and language shifts under British rule
- Tensions leading to the Great Trek

CHAPTER 8: THE GREAT TREK AND NEW COMMUNITIES

- Motivations behind the Voortrekkers' journey
- Clashes and treaties with African polities
- Formation of early Boer republics inland

CHAPTER 9: THE BOER REPUBLICS EMERGE

- Transvaal (South African Republic) and Orange Free State
- Roman-Dutch law, Volksraad, and Afrikaner governance
- Relations with neighboring African communities

CHAPTER 10: DIAMONDS, GOLD, AND THE MINERAL REVOLUTION

- Discovery of diamonds at Kimberley and gold on the Witwatersrand
- Rise of mining towns and migrant labor systems
- Shifts in power and the seeds of future conflict

CHAPTER 11: CONFLICTS AND THE ANGLO-ZULU WARS

- King Cetshwayo and British expansion
- Isandlwana, Rorke's Drift, and the fall of the Zulu kingdom
- Implications for other African polities and colonial rule

CHAPTER 12: TENSION AND THE ANGLO-BOER WARS

- Annexation of the Transvaal and the First Anglo-Boer War
- Gold-driven disputes leading to the Second Anglo-Boer War
- The treaty of Vereeniging and British supremacy

CHAPTER 13: THE UNION OF SOUTH AFRICA

- Formation of a dominion uniting four colonies (1910)
- Tensions between English speakers and Afrikaners
- Limited rights for Black, Coloured, and Indian populations

CHAPTER 14: EARLY 20TH CENTURY CHANGES AND CHALLENGES

- Rise of labor movements and white worker strikes
- Segregation policies and African political beginnings
- Economic impacts of World War I and the Great Depression

CHAPTER 15: AFRIKANER IDENTITY AND NATIONALISM

- Memory of the Anglo-Boer Wars and cultural revival
- The National Party (NP) and Afrikaner Broederbond
- "Poor white" problem and Afrikaner economic empowerment

CHAPTER 16: HARDSHIP, ECONOMY, AND THE INTERWAR YEARS

- *Effects of the Great Depression and Pact Government policies*
- *Industrial growth alongside deepening segregation*
- *Urban migration, township living, and pass law enforcement*

CHAPTER 17: SOUTH AFRICA DURING WORLD WAR II

- *Military involvement in East Africa, North Africa, and Italy*
- *Smuts's leadership, economic boom, and urban expansion*
- *Divide between pro-British whites and Afrikaner nationalists*

CHAPTER 18: POST-WAR SHIFTS AND GROWING DIVISIONS

- *Return of stricter segregation after WWII*
- *National Party victory in 1948 and early apartheid plans*
- *Opposition from African, Coloured, and Indian communities*

CHAPTER 19: SEGREGATION POLICIES BEFORE APARTHEID

- *1913 Natives Land Act and early pass laws*
- *Urban Areas Act (1923) and color bars in industry*
- *Evolution of state control over African mobility and labor*

CHAPTER 20: THE THRESHOLD OF MODERN CONFLICT

- *Formalization of apartheid under D.F. Malan's government*
- *Population Registration, Group Areas, and banned mixed marriages*
- *Growing resistance movements and impending larger struggles*

CHAPTER 1

EARLY SOUTH AFRICA AND THE FIRST PEOPLE

Introduction to Early South Africa

Long ago, South Africa looked very different from today. There were no big cities, no tall buildings, and no farms with fences. Instead, there were open grasslands, forests, and coastlines rich with fish. Early humans wandered these lands, gathering plants, hunting animals, and trying to survive. Over thousands of years, their lives changed slowly. They discovered better ways to hunt and started making more advanced tools.

Archaeologists call the longest period of human history the Stone Age. This age is split into early, middle, and late parts. In South Africa, there is evidence of all these stages. Many of the oldest stone tools in the world have been found in caves and sites across the region, such as Sterkfontein and other locations near Johannesburg. This is why some people call this area "the Cradle of Humankind."

Early Stone Age

During the Early Stone Age, which began more than a million years ago, people made very simple tools. These tools were mostly stones that had been shaped to have a sharp edge. They used them for cutting meat or scraping hides. Archaeologists have found these tools in places like the Vaal River area. These early people probably moved around a lot, following herds of animals and looking for new sources of plants to eat.

Middle Stone Age

Over a long period, humans became better at shaping stones. They learned how to strike off flakes from larger rocks, creating sharper and thinner tools. This period is called the Middle Stone Age, which lasted from about 300,000 to 30,000 years ago. People during this time still lived as hunter-gatherers. They used fire for warmth and cooking, which changed how they ate and lived.

It is believed that during this time, humans began to show more complex behavior. For instance, archaeologists have found pigments, like ochre, which might have been used for body painting or art. There are also signs that people started to think about symbols and maybe even spiritual ideas. Some cave sites along the southern coast of South Africa show that people ate shellfish and other marine foods, which expanded their diet.

Late Stone Age and Emergence of Art

Around 30,000 years ago, the Late Stone Age began. Tools became smaller and more specialized. People made arrowheads and other items that were lighter. The bow and arrow might have appeared during this time. This gave hunters a better chance against quick animals. Also, this period is well-known for rock art, often seen in caves and on rock shelters across South Africa.

These paintings, usually made by the San people (often grouped with the Khoisan), depict animals like elands, and sometimes people dancing or hunting. These artworks let us glimpse their beliefs and their daily lives. Some of these rock paintings might have been linked to spiritual rituals or ceremonies. They used natural pigments from rocks, plants, and charcoal, blending them to create beautiful images.

Environmental Changes

Throughout these ages, the land changed many times. Weather patterns shifted, coastlines moved, and certain animals disappeared, while others thrived. These changes forced early people to adapt. If the weather became drier, they had to move to areas with more water. If the weather became colder, they needed better clothing and shelter. Over thousands of years, these groups spread across South Africa. Some remained near the coast, while others went inland to mountains and grasslands.

Early Human Groups and Lifestyle

During the Late Stone Age, most groups lived in small bands of hunter-gatherers. They had to move around often, following the changes in seasons. Gathering plants was often done by the women, while men usually hunted game. Each person in the group had a role. Older people shared knowledge about the land and hunting methods.

At night, these groups might have slept in caves or in temporary huts made from branches and leaves. Their possessions were few, as they could only carry what they needed when they traveled. However, they had strong social bonds and shared food and resources. They also likely told stories around fires at night, passing down traditions through spoken word.

The Importance of Fire and Tools

Fire changed life in many ways. It let people cook meat, which killed germs and made it easier to eat. Fire also scared away wild animals. Sitting around a fire encouraged social bonds and helped people stay warm in cold weather. Tools, too, continued to improve. Sharp stone tools let them skin animals and butcher meat faster. Over time, they also started working with bones, making needles for sewing together animal hides.

Evidence from Archaeology

Archaeologists have dug in many sites across South Africa to find evidence of these early people. They study layers of sediment, which can be dated using scientific techniques. This dating helps us figure out how old tools and bones are. In some cases, archaeologists have found footprints or even human skeletons. These discoveries show us that early humans were smart, flexible, and skilled at surviving in different environments.

Spiritual Beliefs and Rituals

While we do not have written records for these periods, we can guess about their spiritual lives through art and modern studies of traditional San and Khoikhoi practices. It seems these early peoples believed in a spirit world connected to animals and natural places. They might have had shamans, or spiritual guides, who performed dances and rites to heal people or ask for success in hunting.

One famous type of art is the "trance dance" paintings, where human figures are shown in bent postures, possibly indicating a trance-like state during rituals. Modern ethnographic studies of San groups in the Kalahari region offer clues to how ancient people might have lived, though we have to be careful not to assume that all practices stayed the same over thousands of years.

Changes Leading to Later Periods

Eventually, the Stone Age gave way to new eras, especially when people began to keep livestock and grow crops. But these changes did not happen all at once. For a long time, groups of hunter-gatherers continued their traditional way of life. The introduction of herding and farming came from different parts of Africa or through contact with neighboring groups.

The early periods of South Africa's past are often overlooked, but they are very important. They tell us that humans lived here for an incredibly long time. They adapted to changing environments and found ways to survive and even create beautiful art. This sets the stage for all the history that follows, because later arrivals would meet these ancient traditions and sometimes absorb them, or sometimes drive them away.

CHAPTER 2

THE KHOISAN AND THEIR WAY OF LIFE

Introduction

The term "Khoisan" combines two groups: the Khoikhoi (or Khoi) and the San. Although they share historical and cultural ties, these groups have differences in the way they lived. The San, often called Bushmen in older texts, were primarily hunters and gatherers. The Khoikhoi, sometimes called Hottentots in older texts, were mostly herders who kept sheep and cattle. Over centuries, these groups spread across wide parts of southern Africa.

We should remember that these terms can be general labels. Many smaller groups had their own names and customs. But for simplicity, we use "Khoisan" to refer broadly to the older inhabitants of South Africa before large-scale Bantu migration and European colonization. They had unique languages with click sounds, and their traditions were closely tied to the land.

Origins and Distribution

The San are considered one of the oldest continuous populations of humans on Earth. Genetic studies suggest they have very old lineages, connecting them to the earliest modern humans. Meanwhile, the Khoikhoi also have deep roots but are best known for adopting herding. Some historians think the Khoikhoi began raising livestock around 2,000 years ago, possibly learning from neighboring groups.

Before European arrival, the Khoisan lived across most of what is now South Africa, as well as parts of Namibia and Botswana. They adapted to the different ecosystems, from the dry areas of the Karoo and Kalahari to the lush regions near the coasts. Their deep knowledge of the environment allowed them to find water, hunt game, and gather wild plants in places that might seem harsh to outsiders.

Social Structure and Living Arrangements

The San lived as small groups, usually families. These groups had flexible leadership; decisions were often made through discussion. If arguments got too big, people could simply leave and join another group. This kept life peaceful. The San moved with the seasons, staying near water sources, hunting migrating animals, and gathering plants. They had few possessions so they could travel easily.

The Khoikhoi were also organized in groups or clans, but because they had herds, they stayed in one area longer. They needed good grazing land for their sheep and cattle and sources of water. They set up temporary villages of huts made from branches and mats. When the grass was eaten up, they moved on to fresh fields. The chiefs among Khoikhoi groups were often more influential than San leaders, because they had to manage cattle and decide where to graze them.

Economic Activities

1. **Hunting and Gathering (San):**
    - The San hunted game using bows and arrows. They used poison on arrow tips, made from plants or beetle larvae. This poison could slowly kill an animal, and the hunters would track it until it collapsed.

- Gathering plants was very important, since this often provided most of their daily food. They knew which roots and berries were safe to eat and where to find them.

2. **Herding (Khoikhoi):**

    - The Khoikhoi raised cattle, sheep, and goats. Cattle, in particular, were a sign of wealth and status. They used the milk and meat, and hides for clothing or trade.

    - They might trade livestock or livestock products with neighbors. If they lived near the coast, they might also collect shellfish or fish occasionally.

Clothing and Crafts

Both groups wore simple clothing made from animal skins. The San, who moved often, carried small pouches for holding tools, medicines, or herbs. Women might have worn aprons made from soft animal hide. For cooler weather, they used cloaks or karosses, also made from skins.

They decorated themselves with beads and ornaments made from ostrich eggshell, bones, or seeds. These items could be symbols of beauty or could also mark special events. Ostrich eggshell beads are common findings in archaeological sites, showing how widespread this art form was.

Language and Culture

One of the most striking features of Khoisan languages is the use of click sounds. These clicks are written in modern linguistics with symbols like "!," "/," and "|" to show the different types of clicks. The San have many dialects, each with slight differences in sound. The Khoikhoi also spoke languages with clicks, though some differences set them apart from the purely San dialects.

Storytelling was a huge part of cultural life. Stories passed on knowledge about animals, plants, and the world of spirits. Some stories taught lessons about moral behavior. Others explained why things were the way they were—for example, why certain animals look a certain way or why the sun rises each day.

Religion and Beliefs

Both the Khoikhoi and the San believed in spiritual forces. They held that natural elements like the sun, moon, stars, and certain animals had power. The San believed in a supreme creator or great spirit, and they also saw some animals as having special spiritual energy. Certain dances, like the trance dance, allowed healers or shamans to enter a state where they could heal sick people or communicate with the spirit world.

The Khoikhoi had rituals related to cattle. Since cattle were so important, they often sacrificed animals to please the spirits or to ask for protection from sickness. However, it is important to note that these beliefs could vary greatly from one group to another. Not all Khoikhoi or San groups believed exactly the same thing.

Conflicts and Alliances

Because resources were sometimes scarce, conflicts could happen. However, the San usually avoided large-scale fights by moving away. Between the Khoikhoi and the San, there might have been tensions, especially if livestock grazed on land where the San hunted. Still, trade and intermarriage also occurred, blurring the lines between these groups.

In other times, the Khoikhoi needed good relations with the San to safely pass through certain hunting grounds. They might give gifts or allow San hunters to share in livestock. These alliances were fragile, but they show that Khoisan peoples had many ways of resolving disputes without all-out war.

Contact with Other People

Even before Europeans arrived, Khoisan groups sometimes traded with Bantu-speaking farmers or with other hunters. They might exchange skins, ostrich eggshell beads, or cattle for iron tools, grain, or other goods. With time, some San might have joined Bantu communities, losing their hunter-gatherer lifestyle. Meanwhile, some Khoikhoi might have lived near Bantu villages, sharing grazing land or taking part in markets.

Effects of European Arrival

When Europeans (first the Portuguese sailing along the coast, then the Dutch) started to come to the Cape in the 15th and 17th centuries, they needed fresh meat and water for their ships. At first,

Khoikhoi groups near the Cape traded cattle for beads, copper, or tobacco. But as the Dutch East India Company decided to settle and grow crops, they wanted more land. This eventually led to serious conflicts with the Khoikhoi.

The San, who lived further inland, also came into conflict when settlers moved north and east in search of farmland. The arrival of firearms and organized military units changed everything. The Khoisan could not defend their lands effectively. European diseases, like smallpox, caused large-scale deaths among Khoisan communities, who had no immunity to these new illnesses. This tragic encounter led to the decline of many Khoisan groups, forcing survivors to work on farms or merge with other communities.

Legacy and Modern Understanding

Although we are focusing on history and not modern times in this book, it is worth noting that Khoisan heritage has remained important in South Africa. Rock paintings still stand as a reminder of their ancient presence. Words from Khoisan languages have found their way into modern place names and even everyday speech. Historians and archaeologists continue to uncover more about these societies, correcting the older view that they were "primitive." In reality, they had complex social systems and deep knowledge of the land.

The Long Road to Change

By understanding the Khoisan, we learn that South Africa was never an empty land waiting to be settled by newcomers. People had lived there for thousands of years, shaping the environment and forming cultures that lasted for generations. When outsiders arrived, they met communities with their own customs and languages. This clash laid the groundwork for future struggles over land and resources.

Conclusion of Chapter 2

- "Khoisan" refers to the Khoikhoi (herders) and the San (hunter-gatherers).

- They have lived in southern Africa for thousands of years, with distinct languages and cultures.

- The San were known for their fine rock art and expert hunting skills, often using poison arrows.

- The Khoikhoi herded cattle and sheep, and placed great value on livestock.

- Both groups had rich spiritual beliefs, with dances and rituals tied to nature and the spirit world.

- European arrivals and their demand for land and resources led to the decline of many Khoisan communities.

In the next chapters, we will see how new waves of people arrived from the north, bringing agriculture, iron-working, and new social structures. These Bantu-speaking communities would also shape South Africa's history in major ways.

CHAPTER 3

THE BANTU MIGRATIONS AND NEW SETTLEMENTS

Introduction

Long after the early hunter-gatherers and herders had spread across the region, new groups began moving into the land we now call South Africa. They came with new ideas and skills, such as farming and iron-making. Historians often refer to them as **Bantu-speaking peoples** because they spoke languages that belong to the Bantu family. These languages are still spoken by many communities in South Africa today, such as isiZulu, isiXhosa, Sepedi, Setswana, and many others.

This movement of Bantu speakers into southern Africa was part of a much bigger migration that started far to the north, near the border areas of what is now Nigeria and Cameroon. Over centuries, these communities traveled east and south in search of fertile land and better living conditions. Their arrival changed the region's social and cultural landscape, introducing agriculture, new forms of leadership, and different ways of living.

Origins of the Bantu Migration

The Bantu family of languages covers a huge portion of Africa, from Cameroon and Central Africa across East Africa, and all the way down to South Africa. Scholars believe the earliest Bantu groups practiced both small-scale farming and some herding. They also knew how to work with **iron**, forging tools and weapons that gave them advantages over communities that relied on stone tools.

Nobody is certain exactly why these groups began moving south and east. Some suggest climate changes or growing populations that needed more farmland. Others think internal conflicts or the desire for trade might have pushed them to seek new regions. Likely, there were many reasons, and different groups may have had their own motivations. Over hundreds of years, wave after wave of Bantu speakers settled across much of southern Africa, including the highveld, the coastal areas, and river valleys.

The Journey South

As these groups moved closer to what is now South Africa, they followed routes that led them around the thick forests of Central Africa. Some groups traveled through the eastern parts of the continent, passing through present-day Tanzania and Mozambique, before arriving in the Limpopo River region. Others took more inland routes, coming around the Kalahari area from the northwest. Each path had its own challenges—diseases, wild animals, lack of water, or conflicts with other communities.

By the time they arrived in the area south of the Limpopo River, most Bantu-speaking groups had well-developed techniques for **mixed farming** (growing crops and raising livestock). They also had iron tools like hoes and axes, which made farm work easier and faster. Their cooking pots and metal spearheads changed daily life and hunting practices.

Life in the New Settlements

When Bantu-speaking families found good farmland, they built homesteads or villages. A typical homestead might consist of circular huts made from mud or clay, with thatched roofs. Families usually lived close together, and extended relatives formed small communities. Cattle, goats, and chickens wandered nearby. Crops such as millet, sorghum, and later maize (introduced much later from the Americas, but by other routes) grew in fields around these settlements.

Leadership often centered on a headman or chief, who made decisions for the group. People recognized their chief not just as a ruler but also as a spiritual guide who might perform rituals for rain or protection. In many Bantu societies, there were social structures based on age, gender, and lineage. Young men might have certain duties, such as herding cattle or helping with heavy work, while elders offered counsel.

Impact on the Land

As these new communities spread, they changed the environment. Cropland replaced some grasslands where wild animals roamed. Herding practices also shaped the landscape. Cattle, goats, and sheep needed grazing, so these communities had to manage their livestock carefully, ensuring there was enough pasture and water. Over the centuries, farming took root in many places that once belonged primarily to hunter-gatherers or herders.

The **iron-smelting** process required large amounts of charcoal, so forests were cut down for firewood. This altered the structure of woodlands in certain areas. However, it also meant tools were more plentiful, and people could clear land more effectively. The new arrivals had to balance their resource use to make sure they did not exhaust the soil or the local environment.

Interaction with the Khoisan

Before the Bantu speakers arrived, **Khoisan** groups (the Khoikhoi herders and San hunter-gatherers) had long called southern Africa home. In some areas, the Khoisan and the incoming Bantu speakers lived side by side, trading items such as livestock, skins, or iron tools.

In other areas, conflict arose over land and resources. The newcomers, armed with iron weapons, might have displaced or absorbed local Khoisan groups.

In some regions, **Khoisan** individuals joined Bantu communities. They brought knowledge of local plants, hunting grounds, and water sources. Over time, intermarriage occurred, blending traditions and languages. You can still see Khoisan influences in certain Bantu dialects, especially in the form of click sounds that appear in languages like isiXhosa and isiZulu.

Language and Cultural Exchange

The Bantu languages share many similarities, but they also branched into distinct dialects as people settled in different areas. Over many generations, these dialects changed enough to become separate languages. For example, Northern Sotho (Sepedi), Southern Sotho (Sesotho), and Setswana share a lot in common but also have unique features. Similarly, isiZulu, isiXhosa, and siSwati have click sounds that likely came from Khoisan languages.

Culturally, Bantu-speaking communities practiced **ancestor worship** and believed strongly in a link between the living and the dead. Rituals to honor ancestors were common, as people believed spirits could guide and protect families. Many communities also had special ceremonies for coming of age, marriage, and harvest. Music, dance, and story-telling played vital roles in teaching and preserving their heritage.

Early Social and Political Structures

Most Bantu groups were organized around **chiefdoms**, which were sometimes small and sometimes quite large. A chief or king oversaw the well-being of the people, managed land allocation, and served as the highest authority in disputes. Councils of elders or advisors supported the chief, providing wisdom and experience. Over time, as populations grew, some chiefdoms merged or expanded to form larger kingdoms.

In many cases, a powerful chiefdom owed its strength to the control of cattle, the fertility of its land, or trade connections. Raiding could also occur between rival groups, as they sought to increase their herds or secure new farmland. Yet, trade and cooperation often outweighed conflict because life was easier when groups worked together, shared resources, or intermarried to form alliances.

Farming Techniques and Daily Chores

Farming in these communities was usually done by hand, with simple iron hoes. Women often planted seeds, weeded fields, and harvested crops. Men cleared the land and took on heavier jobs, such as building huts or fence enclosures. Children helped by gathering firewood, looking after animals, or fetching water from the river or well.

The staple crops were cereals like sorghum and millet. These grains could be turned into porridge or beer. Vegetables such as beans and pumpkins also grew well. In some areas, fruit trees thrived. Meat, milk, and blood from cattle and goats gave extra protein in the diet. Cattle were highly prized, not only for food but also for **bridewealth** (lobola), a tradition where a man's family gives cattle or livestock to a woman's family before marriage.

Iron Making and Trade

Iron was central to Bantu life, offering better tools than stone or wood. To smelt iron, communities built **furnaces** using clay, with openings for bellows to blow air inside. Burning charcoal created the high heat needed to melt the iron ore. Skilled workers knew exactly how to control the temperature, and they hammered out impurities to produce usable metal. Iron tips on hoes, spears, or arrows made daily tasks and hunting more efficient.

A surplus of metal goods enabled trade. Bantu communities could exchange iron tools or weapons for salt, beads, or other items from neighboring groups. Over time, the region developed a network of **local trade**, linking coastal and inland peoples. Some historians think items like glass beads or cloth came from far-off places through a chain of merchants, eventually reaching Bantu-speaking farmers in the interior.

Patterns of Expansion

As populations rose, younger men often sought new land to farm or to start their own homesteads. Chiefs might encourage expansion to avoid overcrowding and to gain more tribute (taxes) from new territories. Sometimes, disputes or competition for leadership also pushed groups to break away and move further afield.

This pattern spread Bantu-speaking communities far and wide, leading to many different cultural and linguistic variations. In some areas, smaller chiefdoms stayed relatively isolated, especially in mountainous regions. In others, leaders formed powerful alliances, ruling over thousands of people. By about 1000 CE, large parts of eastern and southern South Africa had Bantu-speaking populations that farmed the land, raised animals, and traded.

Spiritual Beliefs and Practices

Religion for Bantu speakers centered on **ancestors**, who were believed to watch over the living and sometimes meddle in daily affairs. People made offerings or sacrifices to please ancestral spirits or to ask for guidance. These offerings might be small portions of food or drink, or in some rare cases, a slaughtered animal during a bigger ceremony.

Healers or diviners played important roles, using herbs and knowledge of the spirit world to treat illnesses and solve social problems. They interpreted signs, performed rituals, and helped the community maintain balance with the natural and supernatural realms. People believed that good health, rain, and bountiful harvests depended on keeping ancestors and other spirits content.

Conflict and Cooperation with Neighbors

While Bantu communities could be peaceful, they also experienced **conflict**. Raids for cattle or disputes over farmland were not uncommon. In times of hardship—like drought—tensions rose. People blamed one another for misfortune or tried to seize resources to survive. However, war was expensive and dangerous. Many chiefs preferred trade, tribute, or intermarriage to build alliances.

When the Bantu speakers encountered the Khoisan, cooperation sometimes happened if the Khoisan offered valuable local knowledge or specialized hunting skills. Yet, Bantu groups with iron weapons had a military edge that could overpower smaller Khoisan bands. As we saw earlier, some Khoisan joined Bantu societies, blending cultures, while others retreated into more remote areas.

Archeological Clues

Much of what we know about early Bantu settlements comes from **archaeology**. Excavations reveal pottery styles, iron furnaces, and the remains of huts and livestock enclosures. Scientists compare these findings with modern Bantu cultures to guess how people lived centuries ago. They also use dating methods, like radiocarbon dating, to figure out the age of artifacts.

Pottery is especially helpful in tracing the movement of Bantu communities. Certain patterns, shapes, or ways of firing the clay can mark a cultural tradition. By mapping these pottery styles across different regions, researchers see how groups spread and which ones might have shared ideas.

Women's Roles and Responsibilities

In many Bantu societies, **women** had significant responsibilities. They handled much of the daily farming and food preparation. They also raised children and passed on cultural traditions. Some societies recognized female leaders, though it was more common for men to be chiefs. Marriage practices often included polygamy, where a man could have multiple wives if he could support them. Each wife typically had her own hut and farmland to manage.

Women also played a major part in spiritual and social events. Some were respected healers or diviners, while others led dances or gatherings. Their deep connection to the land and family made them vital to the success of the community.

Music, Dance, and Oral Traditions

Bantu speakers had rich **oral traditions**, meaning they passed history and knowledge through spoken stories rather than written records. Elders told tales that taught moral lessons, remembered ancestors, or explained natural events. Skilled storytellers used song, poetry, and even riddles to entertain and educate younger people.

Music and dance were not just for fun; they were also forms of spiritual expression. Drums, rattles, and other simple instruments set rhythms for rituals, harvest celebrations, weddings, or the crowning of a new chief. Dances could be lively or solemn, depending on the event. Through these cultural practices, communities stayed united, and new generations learned the values and customs of their ancestors.

Challenges of Settlement

Life for early Bantu settlers was not always easy. Droughts, floods, or locust swarms could destroy crops. Diseases like **malaria** or sleeping sickness (spread by the tsetse fly) posed threats in some areas. Conflicts with neighboring groups or dangerous wild animals also tested their survival skills. Despite these struggles, their technology (iron tools), social organization, and farming methods gave them the means to adapt.

Over centuries, Bantu communities learned to rotate their crops to avoid exhausting the soil, and they used local herbs to fight illness. Cooperation among families made daily work lighter. If a homestead burned down or was destroyed, neighbors helped rebuild it. During tough times, communities often came together to share food or resources.

The Road Toward More Complex Societies

As these farming societies grew, so did their leadership structures. Some chiefs became more powerful by controlling trade routes or bigger herds of cattle. They collected tribute from smaller groups in exchange for protection or grazing rights. Over time, such chiefdoms might turn into early forms of **kingdoms**. This process was not the same everywhere, and it did not happen overnight. It took generations for leaders to accumulate wealth and influence.

In later centuries, some of these expanding chiefdoms gave rise to well-known states in the region. These included the early forms of what would eventually become polities like the **Zulu**, the **Swazi**, and the **Sotho** kingdoms. But that is a story we will explore in future chapters when we look at how local powers grew and how new challenges shaped them.

CHAPTER 4

THE GROWTH OF EARLY AFRICAN KINGDOMS

Introduction

In the previous chapter, we explored how Bantu-speaking farmers settled across southern Africa. Over time, these communities did not remain small and scattered. Some places witnessed the rise of **early African kingdoms**, which were larger political entities with structured leadership and social classes. Chiefs became kings, managing trade, conflict, and alliances over wide territories. These kingdoms laid important foundations for later societies like the Zulu, Swazi, and Sotho polities, though we will not jump too far ahead into modern times.

Historians piece together this story by analyzing archaeological sites, old oral traditions, and the records of travelers. Although many details remain uncertain, we can see patterns of growth, trade, and power that hint at how certain groups became dominant. In this chapter, we will look closely at how these early states came about, what made them strong, and how they contributed to the ever-changing history of South Africa.

From Chiefdoms to Kingdoms

For a Bantu-speaking community to grow into a kingdom, a few key factors usually had to come together:

1. **Leadership:** A strong leader who could unite various chiefdoms under one rule.
2. **Resources:** Access to good farmland, water, iron ore, or valuable trade items.

3. **Trade Networks:** Connections to trade routes that offered goods like salt, metals, or foreign products.
4. **Military Strength:** The ability to protect one's territory from raids or to conduct raids if needed.

When a chief gained power over multiple groups, he might demand **tribute**, often paid in cattle, crops, or labor. This tribute was used to maintain a royal household, reward loyal followers, and strengthen defenses. As power grew, the ruler might claim religious or spiritual authority, saying he was chosen by ancestors or spirits to lead his people. Over generations, such a system could turn a chiefdom into a kingdom, with a clear hierarchy and sense of identity.

The Role of Cattle and Agriculture

Cattle played a huge role in building wealth and prestige. Kings or powerful chiefs measured their success by how large their herds were. Cattle were not just food; they were a form of currency, a mark of social status, and a way to pay bridewealth. Controlling large herds required planning, skilled herders, and solid security against thieves or wild predators.

Agriculture also allowed for **food surpluses**, meaning that not everyone had to spend all day farming. Some people could specialize in crafts, ironworking, or trade. This specialization fueled the growth of towns or centers where merchants and artisans gathered. Over time, these centers attracted more people, adding to the kingdom's population and production power.

Trade and External Contacts

Although South Africa sits far from some well-known ancient trade centers (like the Swahili Coast in East Africa), there was still a fair amount of movement and commerce. Archaeologists have found evidence that local communities obtained glass beads, cloth, or other imported goods. These items likely came from traders who traveled down from East Africa or made connections through a chain of middlemen over long distances.

In exchange, the southern African groups offered ivory, animal skins, and sometimes gold or other minerals. While not as massive as the trans-Saharan trade in West Africa, these exchanges still gave local rulers a way to access luxury items and display their wealth. Controlling trade routes or mining sites could make a kingdom very powerful.

Early State Formation: The Case of Mapungubwe

One of the most famous examples of an early southern African kingdom is **Mapungubwe**, located near the confluence of the Limpopo and Shashe Rivers (near today's border between South Africa, Zimbabwe, and Botswana). Archaeologists date the rise of Mapungubwe to around the 11th century CE. It grew in power over a couple of centuries, becoming an important center for **trade** and social organization.

At Mapungubwe, people built a **hilltop settlement** for the elite, while commoners lived below. This physical separation shows a clear **class difference**—the leaders had special status and likely claimed religious authority as well. Excavations at Mapungubwe have uncovered gold objects, glass beads, and fine pottery, all indicating trade connections beyond the immediate region. Gold items, in particular, suggest that the kingdom had access to gold ore, possibly traded out to East African ports and beyond.

The rulers of Mapungubwe used their wealth to reinforce their control. This system worked for a time, but by the 13th century, the kingdom began to decline, perhaps due to environmental changes, shifts in trade routes, or political competition. Still, Mapungubwe left a lasting mark on the cultural memory of the region and set a pattern for how a sophisticated kingdom could arise in southern Africa.

Social Hierarchy and Organization

In many of these early kingdoms, society was organized around **kinship** (family and lineage) and loyalty to the ruler. Each family group or clan had its leaders, who owed allegiance to higher chiefs, and all reported ultimately to the king. The king's court might include advisers, generals, religious specialists, and relatives who held positions of power. Women could hold influence behind the scenes, especially royal wives or mothers of princes, though official leadership roles for women were less common.

People typically paid tribute to the king, which might include cattle, grains, or labor. In return, the king was expected to protect them from outside threats and ensure the favor of ancestors. Festivals, ceremonies, and rituals involved the entire community, reinforcing a sense of unity. Music, dance, and costume often played key roles in these gatherings, showing off the kingdom's pride and wealth.

Religion and Spiritual Authority

Just as in smaller chiefdoms, ancestors remained central to the belief system in these kingdoms. However, a king often claimed a special link to powerful ancestors, saying that only he (or his appointed spiritual leaders) could mediate between the spirit world and the people. This gave the king additional authority and might discourage rebellion, since opposing the king could be seen as **offending the spirits**.

Certain shrines or sacred places were reserved for royal ceremonies, possibly on hilltops or near important rivers. The king or religious specialists performed rituals to bring rain, protect the harvest, or ensure victory in warfare. When times were good—such as a good rainy season or success in battle—people thanked the spirits. When times were bad, they looked to the king and priests for an explanation or solution. This spiritual dimension bound the kingdom together.

Other Emerging Centers and Chiefdoms

While Mapungubwe is well-known, other areas in what is now South Africa also saw the rise of more complex societies. Archaeological sites in places like **Thulamela** (in the northeastern part of the country) show the presence of walled enclosures, specialized crafts, and evidence of trade. In the Highveld and KwaZulu-Natal regions, smaller groups organized themselves around powerful chiefs who later grew in influence.

These societies varied in size and organization. Some might have been loosely united chiefdoms, while others were more centralized. Though details can be unclear, it is evident that early state-building was not limited to one region. Wherever resources and good leadership lined up, communities could expand and strengthen.

Military Structure and Defense

For a kingdom to remain stable, it needed a system of defense. Raiding was a common practice, either to capture cattle or to punish disloyal subjects. Armies or regiments might be organized under the king's command, with loyal captains leading groups of warriors. Young men often received some form of **military training** as part of growing up. Weapons included spears, axes, and sometimes bows, though the spear became more prominent in later times.

Fortified towns or natural features, like hills and cliffs, served as defensive positions. Stockades made from wood or stone walls around key settlements offered a layer of protection. People kept watch for invaders, and warning signals—such as drums or horns—could quickly bring the community together. In times of relative peace, the army also served as a symbol of the king's might, deterring would-be attackers.

Economy and Craftsmanship

The economy of these kingdoms relied on a blend of **farming, herding, trade, and craftsmanship**. Blacksmiths who could work iron were highly respected, as they provided essential tools for both agriculture and warfare. Pottery makers, weavers, and woodcarvers produced household goods and decorative items. Skilled artisans might specialize in jewelry-making, especially if gold or copper was available.

Trade with distant regions exposed local artisans to new ideas. They might copy pottery styles from afar or incorporate foreign designs into their own crafts. Over time, each kingdom developed a distinctive art style, revealing its people's creativity and outside influences. This exchange of ideas was another force pulling smaller groups together into larger political and cultural units.

Relations Between Kingdoms

While many of these early kingdoms and chiefdoms coexisted, they could also come into conflict. Powerful leaders sought to control more land, cattle, or trade routes. Sometimes they formed alliances with neighboring rulers, sealed by marriages or mutual defense agreements. Other times, distrust led to raids or open warfare. Victories might lead to the winning side capturing cattle and bringing new subjects under their rule.

However, no single king ever managed to unite the entire region of what is now South Africa before European colonization began to intensify in later centuries. Instead, there were multiple centers of power, each with its own approach to ruling and dealing with neighbors. This balance of rivalry and cooperation shaped the political map of southern Africa for many generations.

Language and Cultural Development

As kingdoms grew, **languages** continued to evolve. Certain dialects might become more prestigious if they were spoken at the royal court. Poets and praise-singers performed at the king's kraal (homestead), celebrating his lineage and achievements. Storytellers, too, kept oral histories of battles, famines, and heroic deeds. Over time, these stories contributed to a sense of identity and unity among the people of each kingdom.

Clothing and adornments also reflected social status. Fine beadwork, intricate hairstyles, or special garments set the royal family apart from commoners. Ceremonial objects—like royal staffs or thrones—became symbols of authority. These objects might be decorated with carvings or patterns that told stories of the kingdom's founders or legendary heroes.

Climate and Environmental Pressures

The success of any kingdom also depended on **climate** and environment. If rains failed, crops would wither, leading to hunger and unrest. Water sources could dry up, forcing people to move or fight over scarce resources. Diseases might sweep through cattle herds, ruining the kingdom's economy. Leaders who failed to prevent or mitigate these crises could lose the trust of their people.

Some kingdoms tried to manage these risks by storing grain or building alliances that allowed them to trade in times of need. Others settled near reliable rivers or areas with decent rainfall. But nature was unpredictable, and even the strongest rulers could face downfall when droughts or epidemics struck multiple years in a row.

The Importance of Oral Tradition

Because most of these kingdoms did not develop writing systems, **oral tradition** was their main way of preserving history. Royal genealogies traced the line of kings back to semi-mythical ancestors. Praise-songs highlighted great victories or wise leadership. Myths explained the origins of the people and the land. This oral heritage fostered a sense of pride and continuity through generations.

At the same time, oral history can shift or become embellished. Details might change to favor one ruler's version of events, or heroic deeds could be exaggerated over time. Modern historians and archaeologists compare oral accounts with physical evidence to build a fuller, more accurate picture. Even so, these stories remain a vital record of the beliefs and achievements of early African kingdoms.

Everyday Life in a Kingdom

Common people in these kingdoms led lives not too different from those in simpler chiefdoms. They farmed, herded cattle, cooked food, raised children, and followed social customs. However, they might also owe regular tribute or labor to the king. They could be summoned to build public works, such as the king's residence, roads, or storage buildings.

Festivals and royal visits were major events. People would dress in their best clothing, present gifts, and enjoy singing, dancing, and drumming. The king or his representatives might use these events to announce new laws, settle disputes, or celebrate a successful harvest. For many, these gatherings offered a break from the daily grind of farm work, reminding them that they were part of a larger community.

Decline or Transformation

In history, kingdoms rise and fall. Factors that could weaken a kingdom included **power struggles**, the death of a strong leader without a clear successor, or invasions by rival states. Environmental crises or changes in trade routes might cause people to leave in search of better opportunities. Some kingdoms fractured into smaller chiefdoms or were absorbed into neighboring powers. Yet, even when a kingdom fell, the cultural legacy lived on in its people.

Centuries later, new powers emerged in different parts of southern Africa, building on older traditions but also forging new paths. For instance, further north, the famous Great Zimbabwe rose to prominence after Mapungubwe's decline, although Great Zimbabwe is located outside present-day South Africa. Still, influences from these great states seeped into the wider region through trade and migration, shaping the course of local history.

Conclusion of Chapter 4

These early African kingdoms show that before large-scale European intrusion, southern Africa had **complex societies** with structured leadership, trade links, and rich cultural traditions. The example of Mapungubwe illustrates how a kingdom can form around trade, resources, and strong leadership. Other regions also saw their own forms of state-building, with kings or chiefs who commanded loyalty and respect.

Understanding this background is vital to seeing how later events unfold. As we continue our journey, we will look at the coming of European explorers, how they made contact with these local powers, and how conflicts and alliances took shape. But for now, we recognize that South Africa had its own dynamic political and cultural landscape well before foreign ships began to arrive in large numbers. These kingdoms left behind stories, art, and traditions that remain part of South Africa's heritage.

CHAPTER 5

THE ARRIVAL OF THE PORTUGUESE EXPLORERS

Introduction

In the late 1400s, European powers were searching for new routes to Asia. Spices like pepper, cloves, and cinnamon were very valuable at this time, and traders in Europe wanted direct access to these goods. They hoped to avoid the long and costly land routes controlled by Middle Eastern traders. Portugal, a small country on the Atlantic coast of Europe, led many of these exploratory voyages. Portuguese explorers began sailing down the west coast of Africa, setting up forts and trading posts along the way. Their goal was to find a way around Africa to reach India and other parts of Asia by sea.

In the process, these explorers reached southern Africa. Though they did not immediately settle large parts of the region, they started making contact with local people, changing the course of South African history. They named places, recorded their impressions in journals, and sometimes clashed with the inhabitants. This chapter looks closely at how the Portuguese arrived, what they saw, and the effects they had on the societies they encountered.

1. Early Portuguese Exploration Efforts

Prince Henry the Navigator

The story begins with Prince Henry the Navigator of Portugal (1394–1460). He was not an explorer himself, but he sponsored many voyages along the African coast. Under his guidance, Portuguese captains and crews learned more about navigation, ocean currents, and how to build sturdy ships known as caravels. These caravels could handle storms better than older ships and sail closer to the wind.

By the mid-1400s, the Portuguese had sailed beyond Cape Bojador and Cape Verde in West Africa. They discovered islands like the Azores and Madeira. Their main interests included gold from West Africa and slaves who were sold into servitude in Europe. Over time, they built forts along the African coast, but they still dreamed of reaching the riches of the East, especially the spice markets of India.

Bartolomeu Dias Reaches the Cape

The big breakthrough came in 1488, when **Bartolomeu Dias** sailed around the southernmost tip of Africa. His voyage proved it was possible to connect the Atlantic and Indian Oceans by sea. Dias called the southern tip "Cabo das Tormentas" (Cape of Storms) because of the fierce weather he faced. However, when he returned to Portugal, King John II supposedly renamed it "Cabo da Boa Esperança" (Cape of Good Hope), highlighting the hope of finding a direct sea route to India.

Dias's journey was remarkable and dangerous. His ships battled heavy winds and rough seas. He went beyond the point where most Europeans had ever sailed. After rounding the Cape, he traveled along the southern coast of Africa, making brief landings. He met local inhabitants, probably Khoisan groups living near the coast, but detailed records of these encounters are limited. Still, Bartolomeu Dias's success opened the way for future voyages.

Vasco da Gama's Voyage to India

Following Dias's achievement, **Vasco da Gama** led a Portuguese expedition in 1497 to reach India by sea. He sailed around the Cape of Good Hope, passing various points along South Africa's coastline, and eventually reached the Indian Ocean. After several stops on the East African coast, he found pilots familiar with monsoon winds who guided him to Calicut (now Kozhikode) in India.

Da Gama's journey was very important for European trade. It confirmed the route around Africa as a viable path to the wealthy cities of the East. Though da Gama did not establish permanent settlements in South Africa, he left a record of Portuguese contacts with coastal peoples. His success inspired other Portuguese voyages in the years to come, some of which interacted more deeply with local groups in southern Africa.

2. Encounters with Coastal Peoples

Trade and Exchange

When Portuguese ships anchored along the South African coast, the sailors often needed fresh water and food supplies. They sometimes traded items like beads, mirrors, or bits of metal with Khoisan communities in exchange for cattle and sheep. These Khoisan people had long practiced coastal herding, fishing, and gathering. To them, the arrival of large European ships must have been strange and possibly alarming.

Early trade between the Portuguese and local groups was limited and could be tense. Misunderstandings about value, language barriers, and cultural differences sometimes led to conflict. The Portuguese often wrote about these encounters in diaries, noting the unusual click sounds in local languages. Over time, some of the Khoisan learned how to bargain for more favorable exchanges, asking for better goods and resisting attempts by the Portuguese to take resources by force.

Conflict and Violence

Not all encounters were friendly. Portuguese explorers carried muskets and cannons, weapons new to southern Africa at the time. Fear and mistrust could spark violence. For example, if the Portuguese tried to seize water supplies or cattle without fair trade, local inhabitants fought back. At times, a few Portuguese sailors were wounded or killed. In response, the Portuguese might fire their cannons or muskets at the shore, causing damage and fear.

These conflicts, while small in scale, set a pattern of uneasy contact. The Portuguese did not plan to settle in South Africa. They were mainly passing through on the way to India or back to Europe. Still, their brief stops mattered. They introduced new goods, displayed new weapons, and left stories behind about people with pale skin arriving from faraway seas.

3. Portuguese Shipwrecks and Castaways

The Dangers of Navigation

The Cape of Good Hope and the nearby waters are well-known for storms, strong currents, and hidden rocks. For many Portuguese ships traveling between Europe and Asia, wrecking along the South African coast became a real possibility. When a ship struck a reef or was destroyed by violent weather, survivors sometimes found themselves stranded. They had to rely on local communities or their own resourcefulness to survive.

These shipwreck stories offer unique glimpses into early contact. While official reports from passing ships can be brief, accounts from castaways are often more detailed because they spent months or even years among local peoples. Some of the Portuguese survivors walked hundreds of miles, hoping to reach other ships or outposts. They encountered various indigenous groups, learned bits of local languages, and adapted to local diets.

Famous Shipwreck Tales

One notable story is that of the **São João**, wrecked near the southeastern coast of South Africa in 1552. Loaded with goods from India—like spices, porcelain, and other valuables—it struck the rocks in bad weather. Many passengers died, but some lived and made their way to shore. Over time, these survivors mixed with local communities. Later, they tried to travel north toward Mozambique, where the Portuguese had established more permanent posts.

Another example is the **Santo Alberto** in 1593, also wrecked on the eastern coast. Survivors again tried to reach Portuguese settlements far away. Some died on the journey, while others managed to survive, often with the help (or occasional hindrance) of local inhabitants. These stories of endurance, hunger, and cultural exchange reveal the deep challenges faced by early sailors.

Cultural Exchanges from Stranding

Castaways who lived with local communities for months or years learned new survival skills. They might share knowledge of European tools, weaponry, or Christianity with the people who hosted them. Meanwhile, they adopted local clothing, learned to hunt or herd, and participated in local rituals. Although these were small-scale interactions, each one wove a thread in the broader tapestry of contact and exchange.

Some survivors eventually made it back to Portugal or to other Portuguese outposts. Their tales spread in Europe, portraying southern Africa as both dangerous and full of potential. They described fierce storms, unfamiliar peoples, and the possibility of hidden riches or new markets. Their stories fed European curiosity about the southern tip of Africa, though no big colonization attempt by Portugal followed at this time.

---

4. Portuguese Influence on African Coastal Towns

The Focus on East Africa and Asia

Portugal's main interest lay further north and east along the Indian Ocean. They built forts and trading stations along the Swahili coast, in places like Mozambique Island, Mombasa, and Sofala. These ports allowed them to control parts of the gold trade from the interior, as well as the movement of spices and other goods. Because of this focus, the Portuguese never established a large, lasting colony in what is now South Africa. They saw it mostly as a stopover point.

However, Portuguese ships did visit the ports of present-day Mozambique and other areas that connected to the interior. Some of the goods traveling down the old trade routes from places like Great

Zimbabwe or its successor states might have reached Portuguese hands. In return, Portuguese items like cloth, beads, and ironware flowed inland. So, indirectly, the presence of Portugal in East Africa affected the economy of regions further south.

Christian Missionaries and Early Writings

A few Catholic missionaries, mostly under royal or church sponsorship, traveled aboard Portuguese ships. They aimed to spread Christianity to the peoples they met, including those in southeastern Africa. While direct missionary work in the far south was rare at this time, some records mention attempts to convert local leaders along the coast or to establish small chapels. These efforts were not as thorough or large-scale as they were in places like the Kongo Kingdom or Ethiopia.

Nevertheless, Portuguese priests and chroniclers wrote down observations about local religions, social systems, and customs. Although these writings were filtered through European perspectives and often biased, they form part of the earliest written records about southern Africa's inhabitants. Researchers today compare them with oral histories, archaeology, and other sources to build a better understanding of the period.

---

5. Consequences for Local Societies

Introduction of New Items and Ideas

Even without permanent Portuguese settlements in South Africa, local peoples encountered new items and ideas. Iron tools were not new to the Bantu-speaking farmers in the interior—these had been part of life for centuries. But Portuguese metal objects like knives, nails, and even small bells might have circulated through coastal trade. Over time, such goods could reach inland chiefdoms, sometimes raising the status of those who owned them.

European cloth, although initially rare, became a prized commodity. It was lighter and differently woven than local cloth or animal skins. Beads, in particular, had a big impact. While people in southern Africa already made and used beads (for instance, from ostrich eggshell), the bright colors of glass beads were seen as exotic and appealing. Chiefs might give these beads as gifts to allies or wear them as symbols of prestige.

Disease and Population Effects

A significant issue was the possible introduction of new diseases. Crew members on Portuguese ships sometimes carried illnesses like smallpox. Although major epidemics connected to the Portuguese are not well-documented in the 1500s for the Cape region, the risk certainly existed. Later waves of European contact would bring large-scale epidemics. Still, the earlier encounters might have spread some unfamiliar sicknesses that local communities had never faced before. This is difficult to confirm from the scant historical records.

Shifts in Power Dynamics

Knowledge of firearms spread gradually through rumors, occasional demonstrations, or trade. Local leaders who witnessed muskets recognized their destructive power. However, the Portuguese were not interested in supplying firearms to communities around the Cape. They preferred to keep their advantage. As time passed, though, the idea of gunpowder weapons would come to influence power balances in the region once other Europeans arrived.

For coastal Khoisan groups that relied on pastoralism (herding sheep and cattle) and trade with passing ships, the presence of Portuguese vessels was sometimes an opportunity, sometimes a threat. If they negotiated well, they could acquire goods. If they angered the visitors or refused demands, they might face violence. This uncertain relationship likely made them cautious, shaping how they dealt with later arrivals from Europe.

6. The Decline of Portuguese Dominance

Competition with Other European Powers

In the 1500s, Portugal was the leading maritime power in Africa and Asia. But in the 1600s, other European nations—like the Netherlands and England—challenged Portuguese sea control. Better-armed Dutch and English fleets started to raid Portuguese possessions, weakening their hold on coastal forts. Over time, the Dutch and English formed their own chartered companies, like the Dutch East India Company (VOC) and the English East India Company, to trade directly with Asia.

These new arrivals had big plans for the Cape region, which they saw as an ideal place to stop for fresh water and supplies. The Dutch, in particular, would soon establish a permanent settlement at the Cape of Good Hope. This would overshadow Portugal's earlier, more limited presence along the southern coast.

Shift in Portuguese Interests

By the early 17th century, Portuguese influence along the southern African coast was minimal, limited mainly to ships stopping for fresh water, or the occasional castaway. Their holdings became centered around Mozambique in southeastern Africa, and other outposts further north. With the decline of their naval supremacy, they could not protect every route around Africa, and the Dutch moved in on important sea lanes.

For South Africa, this meant that the earliest European contact was set to change. While Portuguese ships would still pass by, the next phase of European involvement would come from the Dutch, who brought new ideas about setting up a colony. Portugal's role shifted to a smaller part in the larger drama of southern Africa's history, but their first steps—rounding the Cape—were crucial in opening the region to the rest of the world.

7. Legacy of the Portuguese in South Africa

A Gateway for Other Europeans

Although Portugal never founded a large colony at the Cape, their explorers mapped the coastline and proved the sea route around Africa to Asia. This knowledge spread throughout Europe, inspiring others. It is likely that without Bartolomeu Dias and Vasco da Gama's successful voyages, the Cape might have stayed out of direct European focus for much longer.

The Portuguese also showed that local resources, such as cattle, could be obtained by trade (or force) at certain points along the coast. Their records hinted at the possibility of valuable minerals in the interior (like gold), even if they did not explore deeply into the highveld or coastal plains of South Africa.

Early Cultural Footprints

Portuguese words, place names, and stories filtered into the region. For instance, one theory suggests that the name "Natal," referring to the coast where Da Gama landed on Christmas Day in 1497, comes from the Portuguese word for Christmas ("Natal"). Although official usage of the name Natal came much later, the concept may trace back to that voyage. Beyond place names, the exchange of goods and limited interaction left small but notable marks in local oral traditions.

Conclusion of Chapter 5

The arrival of the Portuguese explorers was a turning point in South Africa's history. Though they did not settle or deeply colonize the region, they revealed its coastline to the wider world. Their occasional contacts with local Khoisan groups were often uneasy, marked by trade, misunderstandings, and sometimes violence. Shipwreck survivors lived with local communities, sharing knowledge and leaving behind remarkable tales.

Most importantly, the Portuguese voyages demonstrated that the Cape of Good Hope was not the impassable barrier some Europeans had imagined. This knowledge paved the way for other European powers, especially the Dutch, to take a stronger interest in establishing a permanent outpost at the tip of Africa. In the next chapter, we will see how the Dutch East India Company (VOC) moved in and changed South Africa's story forever.

CHAPTER 6

DUTCH SETTLEMENT AT THE CAPE

Introduction

By the mid-17th century, the **Dutch** had become a dominant sea power, rivaling and often surpassing the Portuguese in many parts of the globe. They formed the **Dutch East India Company** (known as the VOC, from its Dutch name Vereenigde Oostindische Compagnie) in 1602. This company focused on the lucrative spice trade from Asia, sailing vast distances around Africa to reach places like the East Indies (modern-day Indonesia). Along this long journey, their ships regularly needed fresh water, food, and a place to repair damages.

The Cape of Good Hope stood out as a strategic location. Although Portuguese explorers had discovered and named the Cape nearly two centuries earlier, they had never established a major base there. The VOC recognized that a settlement at the Cape could serve as a refreshment station for passing ships, reducing costs and saving time. This chapter covers how the Dutch established their colony at the Cape, the challenges they faced, and the impact on local people and the environment.

1. The Reasons Behind Dutch Settlement

The Importance of a Refreshment Station

Dutch ships traveling to and from Asia spent many months at sea, risking scurvy and other illnesses due to a lack of fresh produce. Stopping at the Cape allowed them to gather fresh water, vegetables, and fruit. Crews could recover, make repairs, and prepare for the next leg of their journey. Having a permanent station was cheaper and more efficient than relying on chance trades with local Khoisan herders or risky expeditions ashore each time.

Moreover, the Dutch East India Company wanted to keep a close eye on other European ships traveling around the Cape. By establishing a fort, they could control shipping routes, store goods, and defend their interests if needed. The Company leaders saw this as a practical business decision that could pay off in the long run.

Jan van Riebeeck and the First Colony

In 1652, **Jan van Riebeeck**, an employee of the VOC, arrived at the Cape with a small group of settlers. Their task was to create a secure base, build a fort, and start gardens to grow fresh produce. Van Riebeeck's group included a mix of VOC officials, soldiers, and laborers. They landed in Table Bay, where the iconic Table Mountain provided a dramatic backdrop.

Van Riebeeck wrote detailed diaries, describing his efforts to build the **Fort of Good Hope**, set up gardens, and trade with local Khoisan communities for livestock. At first, the settlement was small, just a few wooden or thatched buildings, but it grew steadily. The VOC sent supplies and more personnel from the Netherlands, especially when they saw potential profits in the project.

2. Relations with the Khoisan

Early Trade and Cooperation

Initially, Van Riebeeck aimed for friendly relations with the Khoisan. The Dutch needed cattle and sheep to feed their sailors, and they hoped to buy these animals. They also wanted to learn which local crops grew best and where to find good grazing lands. Khoisan herders, if willing, could be valuable partners.

For a while, some Khoikhoi (Khoi) groups traded livestock with the Dutch, receiving beads, copper, tobacco, and other goods in return. However, the Dutch had a tendency to set fixed prices, which often did not favor the Khoikhoi. Also, they wanted to claim certain tracts of land to grow wheat, grapes, and other produce for their station. This land was used seasonally by the Khoikhoi for grazing. Tension grew when the Dutch started fencing off areas, restricting access to water sources.

Competition for Land and Resources

The Cape region had an important resource: enough rainfall (especially in winter months) to support crops and livestock. The Khoikhoi had long used the plains and valleys for herding, moving from place to place with the seasons. When the Dutch built permanent farms, they blocked these routes. The Khoikhoi who lost grazing land struggled to find enough pasture for their animals.

Clashes began when Khoikhoi groups felt cheated in trade or lost vital water points. The Dutch, with firearms, had a clear military advantage. Over time, the Company justified seizing more and more land, claiming it was "unoccupied" or "unused," ignoring Khoikhoi land-use patterns. This led to a series of conflicts often called the **Khoikhoi-Dutch Wars** or "Khoikhoi-Dutch skirmishes," which happened throughout the later 1650s and 1660s.

---

3. Building the Dutch Colony

The Fort and Early Infrastructure

The first priority for the Dutch was building a fort to protect themselves. They chose a spot not far from Table Bay's shore, where ships could anchor. At first, this was a simple wooden structure, but over time, they built more permanent walls with stone and mud bricks. The fort served as a storehouse for food and ammunition, and as the base for Company operations.

Van Riebeeck also set up gardens near the Liesbeek River. He and his men experimented with European seeds—like cabbages, carrots, onions, and fruit trees—to see what would grow in the local climate. Success varied, but they found certain crops did well, especially with proper irrigation. The aim was to supply ships with enough produce to prevent scurvy (a disease caused by vitamin C deficiency) and keep the crews healthy.

Free Burghers and Expansion

To boost production, the VOC decided to allow certain Company employees to become **free burghers** (free citizens). This meant they could leave Company service and receive land from the VOC under certain conditions. In return, they had to farm and sell produce mainly to the Company at fixed prices. This policy started in 1657 and led to an expansion of farmland around the settlement.

The free burghers established small farms along the Liesbeek River, gradually pushing the Khoikhoi away. They often used hired labor or slaves to work the fields. The VOC liked this arrangement because it did not have to pay all the costs of farming, yet it could still control the market. Over time, a class of **Dutch settlers** grew, some of whom prospered and expanded their farms, forming the roots of what would become the Afrikaner (or Boer) community.

---

4. The Introduction of Slavery

The Need for Labor

One challenge for the Dutch settlers was finding enough laborers to do the heavy work of plowing, building, and tending livestock. Some

Khoikhoi worked for the Dutch, but many resisted permanent employment. The Dutch also had soldiers and Company servants, but these men were not always eager farmers. As the settlement grew, the VOC turned to **slave labor** to fill the gap.

The first slaves arrived at the Cape in 1658, captured from a Portuguese slave ship. Later, the Dutch imported slaves from their colonies in the East Indies (like Indonesia), from Madagascar, and from parts of East Africa. Over time, a diverse slave population formed, speaking different languages and having different cultural backgrounds. They labored in fields, worked as house servants, and carried out many tasks that kept the colony running.

Slave Life and Hardships

Slavery at the Cape was often brutal. Slaves had few rights and could be punished or sold. Families were split up if it suited their owners. Some slaves rebelled or tried to run away, but the Dutch authorities set up strict rules and patrols to capture escapees. Despite these hardships, slaves formed communities, shared cultural practices, and found ways to survive.

Many slaves worked on Company farms or in private farms owned by free burghers. Others worked in town, building roads, unloading ships, or serving as craftsmen. Female slaves also performed domestic chores, cooking, cleaning, or caring for children in settler households. Over time, the mixing of slave, Khoisan, and European backgrounds shaped the cultural landscape of the Cape, leading to new creole languages and cultural expressions.

5. Social Life in the Early Colony

The Settler Community

Life at the Cape station was not always easy. Supplies from Europe could be delayed, leading to shortages. Diseases like dysentery, smallpox, and malaria caused deaths among settlers, slaves, and local peoples. Settlers often lived in simple houses made of clay and thatch, though some wealthier individuals built sturdier homes as time passed.

A small group of officials, including Van Riebeeck and later governors, oversaw the colony. They had significant power: they decided land grants, set tax rates, and enforced Company rules. Free burghers sometimes felt restricted by the Company's tight economic control. Still, many recognized the opportunities: farmland in the Cape's fertile valleys could yield good harvests, and the demand for produce from passing ships was high.

Religion and the Church

The Dutch Reformed Church became the main religious institution for settlers. Ministers came from the Netherlands, baptizing children, marrying couples, and preaching sermons. Services were often held in small, simple buildings in the early years. The Church also tried to teach the Christian faith to slaves and indigenous peoples, though with limited success at first. Over time, new congregations appeared as the settlement expanded into outlying farms.

Religious festivals, like Christmas and Easter, gave the settlers a sense of community and continuity with their European roots. However, day-to-day life was consumed by farming chores, business deals, and coping with the colony's hardships. In private, many settlers missed their homeland's comforts, but they adapted as best they could, relying on each other in times of need.

Cultural Exchanges and Language

From the earliest days, the Cape was a meeting place of many cultures: Dutch, Khoisan, slaves from Asia and Africa, and occasional visitors from England, France, or other nations. Although the VOC tried to maintain a Dutch identity, the daily mixing of languages and customs led to gradual changes. Over many generations, a new language—what we now call **Afrikaans**—would grow, influenced by Dutch, Khoisan, Malay, Portuguese creole, and other tongues. But in the 1600s, this process was just beginning.

---

6. Conflict and Expansion

The First Khoikhoi-Dutch War (1659-1660)

Tensions over land and resources soon flared into open conflict. In 1659, Khoikhoi herders clashed with Dutch free burghers along the

Liesbeek River. The Khoikhoi felt their grazing lands were being taken unfairly, while the Dutch insisted they had the right to fence off farms for crops. Fighting erupted, and Van Riebeeck organized armed patrols. The Dutch, using muskets, drove off Khoikhoi attackers.

In 1660, both sides agreed to a peace settlement, but the Dutch made it clear they would not abandon their farms. The Khoikhoi who lived close to the colony found themselves in a difficult position—losing ancestral grazing lands or being forced to do business on Dutch terms. Many moved further inland, seeking safer areas. This pattern repeated itself in the following decades.

Subsequent Encroachments

As the colony grew, new farms sprang up beyond the first settlement. Free burghers moved into the interior, sometimes receiving permission from the VOC, sometimes just staking out land on their own. Conflict with local Khoikhoi or San (Bushmen) groups flared up repeatedly. The more the Dutch advanced, the less room there was for traditional herding or hunting.

For the Dutch, expansion made sense. They needed new lands to raise crops and livestock. But for the indigenous peoples, it meant displacement, loss of resources, and exposure to diseases. Over time, some Khoikhoi communities disintegrated, their numbers reduced by smallpox epidemics (particularly severe in 1713 and later) and continual loss of land.

---

7. Governance and Company Control

The Role of the Governors

After Van Riebeeck's term ended in 1662, new governors were appointed by the VOC to run the Cape colony. They followed instructions from the Heeren XVII, the Company's board of directors in the Netherlands. The governors had to balance the Company's demands (like producing enough fresh supplies for passing ships) with the settlers' needs (like more land and freedom). Not all governors agreed on how to handle local conflicts or economic policies, so the colony's management could be inconsistent.

Some governors tried to regulate the sale of alcohol or the treatment of slaves. Others cared more about profit. Corruption was not uncommon; officials might use their position to grab land or trade privileges. Still, the VOC's rules shaped daily life: farmers had to sell produce to the Company at fixed prices, and imports or exports required special permission.

The Growing Influence of Free Burghers

Over time, the **free burgher** population increased. Some married locally, including marriages to slave women who had been freed (manumitted). Their children, often called **mestizos** in some records, added to the colony's diverse population. As farms expanded, these burghers began to form a distinct community. They relied less on the VOC for direct support and began to resent certain Company monopolies or taxes.

These settlers developed a self-reliant spirit, especially those who moved further inland, away from the direct oversight of Company officials. Many raised cattle, hunted game, and traded with indigenous peoples on their own terms. This laid the groundwork for a frontier society, where independent farmers (boers) saw themselves as different from the urban, company-focused leaders in Cape Town.

8. The Arrival of Other Europeans

Huguenots and Other Immigrants

By the late 1600s, the Dutch East India Company allowed some other Europeans to settle at the Cape. A notable group was the **French Huguenots**, Protestants fleeing religious persecution in France. They arrived in the 1680s, bringing wine-making skills that became important in the Western Cape. Although they were encouraged to adopt Dutch language and customs, they left a lasting mark, especially in place names and the local wine industry.

There were also a few Germans, Swedes, and others who came under VOC contracts. In time, these groups blended into the Dutch-speaking community, becoming part of the emerging Afrikaner identity. Cape Town gradually became a small but cosmopolitan port, with sailors, traders, and travelers from around the world passing through.

Social and Cultural Changes

With various European immigrants, enslaved people from Asia and Africa, and local Khoisan communities, the Cape was a melting pot of traditions. New dishes appeared, mixing Asian spices with local produce. Clothing styles varied, depending on status and origin. Over time, slaves who gained freedom sometimes formed neighborhoods in or near Cape Town, adding to the area's multicultural feel.

Yet, social divisions were strict. **Racial classifications** began to shape laws and customs, with Europeans (mainly the Dutch) holding the top position, free non-Europeans in a less privileged space, and slaves having the fewest rights. Khoisan people, too, were placed under heavy legal restrictions. This system, though less formal than what would come in later centuries, started to create a society divided along color lines.

9. Economic Activities in the Dutch Cape

Farming and Wine Production

One of the VOC's main goals was to supply fresh produce and meat to its ships. Wheat fields, vineyards, and gardens sprang up around the settlement. French Huguenots contributed wine-making techniques, leading to an early wine industry in Stellenbosch, Franschhoek, and Paarl. These regions remain famous for wine even today. Farmers also raised cattle and sheep, selling them to the Company. Over time, a small export market developed for wine and wheat, although the VOC tried to keep tight control over prices.

Hunting and Ivory Trade

Early settlers and Khoisan hunters supplied meat from wild animals such as eland, springbok, and other game. As frontiersmen moved further inland, they encountered elephants, whose tusks could be sold for ivory, a valuable commodity. Some settlers specialized in hunting elephant or trading for tusks with African communities. This was the start of a long exploitation of wildlife, which would intensify in later eras.

Town Growth and Services

Cape Town itself became a small hub for ship repairs, blacksmithing, carpentry, and other crafts. Taverns, bakeries, and shops served sailors and locals. The VOC built a hospital for sick crew members. Some free burghers found work in the town rather than on farms, opening businesses or serving as artisans. Over time, new buildings appeared, including a church, official residences, and warehouses. By 1700, Cape Town had a few thousand residents, a mix of Europeans, slaves, and freed people of color.

---

10. Legacy of the Dutch Arrival

A New Society Takes Shape

The Dutch settlement at the Cape laid the foundations of a society that would evolve into modern-day South Africa's diverse population. The mix of European settlers, enslaved people from around the globe, and indigenous communities created a complex cultural tapestry. Languages blended, new traditions arose, and social hierarchies formed. Over centuries, this would lead to unique identities, including the emergence of the Afrikaner people and the development of the Afrikaans language.

Long-Term Effects on Indigenous Peoples

The indigenous Khoisan populations suffered greatly under Dutch expansion. Many lost their land, cattle, and freedom. Diseases like smallpox killed large numbers, and the survivors were often forced into labor or pushed to marginal lands. Dutch colonization also influenced Bantu-speaking communities further east, setting the stage for future conflicts as European settlers moved inland. This was the start of a long history of dispossession and struggle for South Africa's first peoples.

Setting the Stage for Future Developments

By the early 1700s, the Cape settlement had become an important stopover for Dutch ships. The VOC continued to rule firmly, but cracks were showing. Settlers complained about Company monopolies and wanted more independence. Over time, some farmers moved far from the Cape's reach, forming new communities in the interior. These developments foreshadowed bigger changes ahead, including the arrival of the British and the push into the heart of southern Africa.

CHAPTER 7

BRITISH INFLUENCE AND THE CAPE COLONY

Introduction

By the late 1700s, European struggles for power had spread across the world's oceans. The Dutch East India Company (VOC), which had founded the Cape Colony in 1652, was weakening due to financial troubles and conflicts in Europe. Great Britain, rising as a major naval power, eyed the Cape as a key stopping point on the route to India and other parts of its growing empire. This chapter explores how the British first occupied the Cape, how they later took permanent control, and how their governance affected local societies—both European settlers and indigenous peoples.

We will look at the reasons behind Britain's interest in the Cape, the changes introduced under British rule, and the tensions that arose. These tensions laid the groundwork for further movements by some Dutch-speaking colonists, who later became known as Boers or Afrikaners. By the end of this chapter, we will see that British influence forever altered the character of the Cape Colony, creating both new opportunities and new conflicts.

1. The Turbulent Late 1700s

European Rivalries and the Dutch Decline

In the late 18th century, the Netherlands found itself caught in wars involving France and Britain. The once-powerful Dutch Republic faced internal strife and external threats. The Dutch East India Company itself was nearly bankrupt from mismanagement and the high cost of protecting trade routes. The Cape Colony, although important for supplies and refreshment, was expensive to maintain.

Across the sea, Britain watched these developments closely. Britain and France were locked in a global struggle, fighting battles in Europe, the Americas, India, and elsewhere. For the British, controlling the Cape would protect their sea route to India. They feared that if France took over the Netherlands or influenced it, France might gain the Cape and block British ships.

French Revolutionary Wars and the Cape

The French Revolution began in 1789, causing upheaval across Europe. Soon, the new French government was at war with other European monarchies. The Netherlands was invaded, and a pro-French regime took power, creating what was called the Batavian Republic. Britain suspected French allies might use Dutch ports and colonies—like the Cape—to harm British trade. Thus, Britain decided to act preemptively.

In 1795, Britain sent a fleet to the Cape. The local Dutch authorities were unsure how to proceed since their homeland was under French pressure. Faced with superior British naval power, the Cape's governor capitulated. This was the **first British occupation** of the Cape, though it was initially meant as a temporary measure. The British would leave if peace returned to Europe and the colony was no longer a strategic risk.

2. The First British Occupation (1795–1803)

Arrival of the British

When British forces arrived in Table Bay, some local Dutch colonists did not know who truly governed them: the old Dutch Republic, the new Batavian Republic, or none at all. The British, well-armed and organized, quickly forced the VOC officials to surrender. Although there was some minor resistance, it did not last long. The British then set up a military administration under General Sir James Henry Craig and, later, General Dundas.

These officials promised that local laws and customs would be respected. The Dutch colonists could keep their land. However, the overall authority now rested with the British Crown. The British aimed to maintain stability, continue trade, and ensure that ships sailing for India could safely refresh at the Cape.

Changes in Administration

During this first occupation, the British made moderate changes. They improved the management of the port, tried to reduce corruption, and reorganized the local militia. Some existing Dutch laws stayed in effect, but the British gradually introduced their own legal ideas, like the principle of "liberty of all religions," which was already familiar to the Dutch but framed in a more British style.

Despite these shifts, the British were not overly harsh on the colonists. They saw the Cape as a useful naval base rather than a place for large-scale British settlement. The local Dutch-speaking population continued many of its usual practices—farming, trading, and employing enslaved people. Yet, the seeds of future cultural and legal change were sown. English started to appear in official documents, and British officials sometimes clashed with Dutch free burghers over taxes or trade policies.

Return to Dutch Rule (1803)

In 1802, Britain and France (and their allies) signed the Treaty of Amiens. One term of this temporary peace agreement was that Britain would hand the Cape back to the Batavian Republic (the Dutch state under French influence). In 1803, the British withdrew, and the **Batavian administration** took over. This new Dutch government tried to implement reforms at the Cape, such as modernizing the legal system and encouraging agriculture. However, the peaceful interlude did not last. War broke out again between Britain and France in 1803, and soon the Cape was back in British sights.

---

3. Permanent British Takeover (1806)

The Second Occupation

In 1806, the British returned with a larger force, capturing the Cape once more after the Battle of Blaauwberg. This time, Britain did not intend a temporary hold. The Napoleonic Wars (in which Napoleon Bonaparte led France against much of Europe) prompted Britain to secure key strategic points. Realizing the Cape was crucial to its global trade, Britain took formal possession. The Dutch governor surrendered, and the colony became a British possession.

In 1814, this became official through an Anglo-Dutch treaty, where the Dutch ceded the Cape to Britain in exchange for financial compensation. The **Cape Colony** was now firmly under British rule, marking the start of deeper changes in governance, law, and society.

Early British Administration

The British installed governors who reported to London. At first, these governors followed a pattern similar to the earlier period:

trying to keep peace, ensure stable food supplies, and protect the shipping route. Over time, however, they began reshaping the colony's legal and cultural systems to mirror British standards. This included introducing British currency, changing court procedures, and encouraging the use of English in official matters.

The local Dutch-speaking settlers, commonly called **Boers**, found these changes unsettling. They were used to their own Dutch-Reformed traditions, Roman-Dutch law, and a more flexible local governance. Although the British recognized Roman-Dutch law in principle, its practice gradually merged with British legal ideas. These developments set the stage for mounting dissatisfaction among segments of the colonial population.

4. Shifts in Law and Society

Language Policies and Administration

One of the most visible changes was the **official use of English**. Government notices, court proceedings, and education in government-sponsored schools began shifting from Dutch to English. While many Boers resented this, some wealthier colonists adapted by learning English, especially those near Cape Town who had business connections.

Local courts moved closer to the British model, with procedures that seemed strange to Dutch farmers from the countryside. They found it harder to represent themselves or understand new legal rules. This language and cultural gap fueled a feeling of alienation, especially among those who lived far from the capital.

The Position of Enslaved People

Under British rule, certain improvements appeared for enslaved individuals. Britain, influenced by growing anti-slavery sentiments at home, began to regulate the slave trade more strictly. In 1807, the British Parliament ended the **slave trade** across the empire (though not slavery itself). This meant no new enslaved people could be legally imported into the Cape Colony. Existing slaves remained in bondage, but the supply of new slaves dwindled.

Later, British authorities also passed the **Amelioration Laws**, which gave enslaved people some limited protections. For instance, they set restrictions on how severely owners could punish slaves. They also required a basic level of food and clothing. To many slaveholders in the colony, these laws seemed like unwelcome meddling in their affairs. To enslaved people, these measures offered small but meaningful relief, though it was far from actual freedom.

Missionaries and Education

British missionary societies, like the **London Missionary Society**, arrived with a commitment to spread Christianity and education, including to indigenous people and the slave population. They built mission stations, taught reading and writing, and sometimes acted as advocates for the rights of marginalized groups. Missionaries also tried to convert Khoikhoi and other Africans. While some local communities welcomed missionaries for help with schooling or assistance in disputes, others remained cautious, fearing a loss of traditional beliefs.

Boer farmers often viewed missionary involvement with suspicion. They worried that missionaries would encourage slaves or Khoikhoi laborers to question settler authority. Moreover, some missionaries openly criticized harsh treatment of workers on farms. These differing outlooks worsened tensions between parts of the Dutch-speaking rural population and the British colonial establishment.

5. Frontier Conflicts and Expansion

Eastern Frontier Challenges

Even before the British arrival, the eastern frontier of the Cape Colony—near the **Fish River** in the present-day Eastern Cape—was a hot spot for clashes between European settlers and Xhosa communities. The Dutch had tried to push the frontier eastward, running into well-organized African chiefdoms. After 1806, the British inherited these **frontier tensions**.

The Xhosa and other Nguni-speaking peoples farmed and herded in the region. They resisted colonial encroachment, leading to a series of **Frontier Wars** (sometimes called the Xhosa Wars). The British sent troops to protect settler farms and attempted to create boundary lines, but disputes continued. Raiding, cattle theft, and violent reprisals became a grim cycle. Over time, the British set up garrisons, built roads, and encouraged new settlers—many of them British—on the eastern frontier to strengthen control.

British Immigration Schemes

To solidify their hold, British authorities began bringing more English-speaking settlers. In 1820, the famous **1820 Settlers** arrived—about 4,000 British subjects settled in places like **Albany**. The government offered them land, tools, and financial help, hoping they would form a buffer against Xhosa communities. These settlers faced their own struggles with poor soil and conflict, but they introduced more English culture and language to the colony.

For Boer farmers already living in the region, this influx of outsiders added another layer of competition for good land. As Britain extended its influence along the frontier, the local African chiefdoms felt increased pressure. A pattern of wars, treaties, and broken agreements would continue for decades, shaping relations between the colony and the various African polities east of the Cape.

6. The End of Slavery (1834–1838)

The Emancipation Act

The biggest shock to Cape society under British rule was the **Slavery Abolition Act** of 1833. This Act, passed by the British Parliament, took effect in 1834 across the empire. It declared that slavery would end, though there was a four-year period of "apprenticeship" in some colonies, including the Cape, to ease the transition. During apprenticeship, formerly enslaved workers were still bound to their owners but with slightly improved conditions. Full freedom was finally granted in 1838.

To many Boer farmers, slavery was central to their economic survival. Although not all farmers owned slaves, those who did relied heavily on this form of labor. The prospect of losing their enslaved workers angered them, and the compensation offered by Britain was seen as insufficient. Worse still, the payments were complicated to claim, as owners had to travel to London or use agents there to get the funds. Many colonists felt cheated.

Social Ramifications

When emancipation became reality in 1838, thousands of former slaves took their freedom. Some stayed on as paid laborers, but many left their old farms in search of better conditions. The labor system of the colony shifted, though not drastically overnight. Wealthy landowners tried to tie workers to farms through **long-term contracts** or **passes** that controlled movement. However, the principle of slavery as a legal institution was gone.

The end of slavery was a moral victory for missionaries and reformers, who saw it as progress. But for the conservative Boer farmers, it was a sign that the British government interfered too much, favoring the rights of laborers over the property rights of slaveholders. This dissatisfaction contributed to a growing desire among many Boers to seek new lands beyond British control.

7. Rising Discontent Among Boer Settlers

Dislike of British Authority

By the 1830s, various British policies—from legal reforms to the end of slavery—convinced a sizeable portion of Dutch-speaking settlers that British rule was no longer tolerable. They resented the push toward English in government and courts, the missionary activity that criticized their treatment of workers, and the new laws that gave indigenous people and free laborers more rights.

These farmers, sometimes called **Trekboers** (wandering farmers), had been moving north and east for years, living far from the Cape administration. They had formed a hardy frontier culture. Used to minimal government interference, they disliked the stricter British presence on the frontier. They felt Britain's policies did not respect their independence or their Calvinist beliefs, which many used to justify rigid social hierarchies.

Economic and Cultural Factors

Beyond slavery, some Boers faced financial struggles. Expanding farms in arid regions required more investment. Conflict with African chiefdoms disrupted trade and security. British taxes and regulations felt heavy-handed. At the same time, these Boers maintained a strong cultural identity tied to their Dutch heritage and the Dutch Reformed Church. They saw British rule as alien and meddling.

Stories also spread of fertile lands far to the north, where Boer families could farm and herd freely without British interference. Some traveling merchants and hunters told of grazing lands beyond the **Orange River** or near the **Vaal**. These tales added to the idea that relocation could bring a fresh start. Thus, a movement was brewing, later known as the **Great Trek**. But that major development is the focus of our next chapter.

8. The Cape Under British Rule: Broader Impact

Changes for Indigenous Peoples

Under British administration, the Cape Colony gradually expanded its borders. This meant more land seizures from the Khoikhoi, San, and Xhosa communities. Though the British government passed laws like Ordinance 50 (1828), which aimed to give free people of color and Khoikhoi more legal equality, the actual impact was mixed. On paper, Khoikhoi could move freely and sign labor contracts as they wished. In practice, many faced discrimination, low wages, and harsh living conditions on white-owned farms.

For African chiefdoms on the eastern frontier, repeated wars with the British left lasting scars. Some leaders signed treaties that ceded territory or limited their autonomy. British forts and new settler towns appeared, creating a multi-sided struggle for land and resources that shaped the region long after this era.

The Growth of Cape Town and Infrastructure

Under the British, **Cape Town** continued to develop as a port. More British merchants arrived, building warehouses, shops, and modest factories. Roads and postal services improved, at least in the more settled western districts. Shipping traffic increased, and the colony's economy partly shifted from being just a refreshment station to a more complex society that exported wine, wheat, and other goods. The British also introduced banks and other financial institutions, modernizing aspects of commercial life.

Yet, outside of major towns, living conditions remained rural and frontier-like for many. Long distances, poor roads, and limited technology made life tough. Communication with distant farms was slow. Disease outbreaks, such as smallpox, continued to devastate indigenous populations at times. Despite the British presence, the Cape Colony was still a frontier society with deep divisions of class, culture, and race.

9. Prelude to the Great Trek

Growing Tensions

By the early 1830s, discontented Boers openly discussed leaving the colony. They held meetings among themselves, drafted "memorials" to the British authorities outlining their complaints, and some small groups began moving north in scouting expeditions. They found that life beyond the colony's official borders was not simple either, as powerful African kingdoms—like the Ndebele under Mzilikazi—controlled certain areas. But the desire for autonomy drove them onward.

Some of these Dutch-speaking settlers believed they had a God-given right to settle lands they deemed "empty," although these lands were usually inhabited or claimed by African communities. They felt that dealing with these communities was a lesser challenge than dealing with British officials, because they could negotiate or fight on their own terms rather than obey laws they disliked.

Ideological Undercurrents

A deep religious conviction spread among some Boers, who saw themselves as a chosen people in a "promised land." Though not all participants in the upcoming Great Trek held extreme views, a sense of manifest destiny grew. The end of slavery was a major spark, but the issues ran deeper—cultural identity, land hunger, and resentment of British authority. The Great Trek would be an attempt to build a society that fit the Trekkers' values, free from external interference.

At this point, the stage is set for the mass migration that would reshape South African history in the 19th century. Chapter 8 will detail the **Great Trek**, exploring the motivations, key leaders, routes taken, and the conflicts that arose between Trekkers and African polities in the interior.

CHAPTER 8

THE GREAT TREK AND NEW COMMUNITIES

Introduction

The **Great Trek** was a key event in South African history. Beginning in the mid-1830s, groups of Dutch-speaking colonists (Boers) left the Cape Colony in large numbers. They traveled in ox-drawn wagons, pushing northward and eastward into regions controlled by powerful African polities. These migrating farmers hoped to escape British rule, maintain their way of life, and find fertile lands where they could form independent communities.

Chapter 8 explores the reasons behind this migration, the main leaders, the challenges encountered, and the communities that the Trekkers founded. We will see how their movement sparked conflict and negotiation with various African groups, how it shaped political boundaries, and why it holds a central place in the story of Afrikaner identity.

1. Reasons for the Great Trek

Discontent Under British Rule

As we saw in the previous chapter, many frontier Boers felt that British policy at the Cape restricted their freedom. They disliked new laws that protected the rights of **Khoikhoi** workers or freed enslaved people. They also felt the British courts were unfair, especially when missionaries supported complaints from indigenous laborers against Boer farmers. The final blow came with the abolition of slavery in 1834–1838, which many Boers saw as a direct assault on their livelihoods and a moral code that justified their control over enslaved labor.

Additionally, some Boer families were deeply religious, believing they had a covenant with God. They felt they were called to live by their own rules, free from British interference. Tales of fertile lands beyond the Orange and Vaal Rivers inspired them. They believed they could farm, herd cattle, and govern themselves without the constraints of the Cape authorities.

Economic Motivations

Economic factors also played a role. The arid or semi-arid lands in the northern reaches of the colony were not ideal for intense farming, and the better lands near the coast or in the southwestern districts were largely taken. Some Boers faced debt or struggled to compete with British merchants in Cape Town. By moving inland, they hoped to secure enough grazing land for livestock, find new hunting opportunities, and avoid high taxes or fees.

For these reasons, the Great Trek was not a single migration but a series of treks, each led by different groups and leaders who had common grievances. Between 1835 and the early 1840s, thousands of Boers (estimates vary) traveled into what is now the interior of South Africa, crossing major rivers and mountain passes in search of a fresh start.

---

2. Organization and Leaders

Commandos and Voortrekkers

Those who took part in the Great Trek called themselves **Voortrekkers** (pioneers). They traveled in groups known as "treks," often organizing themselves under elected leaders and councils. Each trek set out with wagons loaded with supplies: food, blankets, tools, weapons, and Bibles. Men, women, and children all took part, along with any laborers or servants (often of Khoikhoi or mixed descent) who chose or were obliged to follow them.

To defend themselves, the Voortrekkers formed **commandos**, groups of armed men skilled at shooting and riding. They had flintlock muskets and sometimes small cannons. In unknown territory, they had to be ready for conflicts with local communities who might see them as invaders. The commandos also hunted game on the way, gathering food when supplies ran short. Their wagons were arranged in a protective circle (a laager) at night, where families slept inside or near them for safety.

Key Figures

Some of the well-known leaders include:

- **Piet Retief**: A key figure in negotiating with African chiefs, especially in the Natal area. He led a group that aimed to settle in the fertile lands near the coast.
- **Andries Hendrik Potgieter**: Led treks into the northern interior, clashing with the Ndebele led by Mzilikazi. He helped establish communities around the upper Vaal River.
- **Gerrit Maritz**: Often worked alongside Retief. He played a role in the early formation of Boer governance structures during the trek.
- **Andries Pretorius**: Emerged as a prominent leader later, known for his role in battles against the Zulu kingdom and for organizing new Boer republics.

These individuals were not always united. Different groups split or came together depending on personal loyalties, territorial disputes, and interactions with African leaders. Yet, they shared the goal of forming self-governing communities where they could preserve their language, religion, and social practices.

3. Conflicts and Negotiations with African Polities

The Ndebele under Mzilikazi

One of the first major obstacles the Voortrekkers faced was the **Ndebele** kingdom of Mzilikazi in the region north of the Vaal River. Mzilikazi was a formidable ruler who had built a strong state. His forces used military tactics similar to those of the Zulu, with regiments (amabutho) and fast, coordinated attacks. When Boer groups entered his territory without permission, clashes erupted.

Leaders like Andries Potgieter formed alliances with some local chiefdoms who were enemies of the Ndebele. They combined forces against Mzilikazi, defeating his warriors in a series of battles in 1836–1837. Pushed further north, Mzilikazi eventually relocated his kingdom into what is now southwestern Zimbabwe. This opened the highveld for Boer settlement but sowed tensions with other African communities who questioned the Trekkers' claims to land.

The Zulu Kingdom

A major confrontation arose in **Natal**, where the powerful **Zulu kingdom** ruled under King Dingane (after the death of King Shaka and then King Mpande, leadership transitions took place, but Dingane was key in the early 1830s). Piet Retief led a group of Voortrekkers seeking farmland near the coast. He tried to negotiate with Dingane, promising not to settle without the king's agreement.

In early 1838, Dingane invited Retief and his delegation to his kraal (royal homestead). After a ceremony, Dingane accused them of various offenses and ordered their capture. Retief and his men were killed, an event that stunned the rest of the Trekker community. Zulu warriors attacked Boer camps along the rivers, leading to the deaths of many women, children, and settlers in a devastating conflict known to the Boers as **Weenen** (the Place of Weeping).

Battle of Blood River

The Boers regrouped under Andries Pretorius, seeking revenge. On December 16, 1838, a Boer commando clashed with a large Zulu force at the **Ncome River**. Due to their defensive laager of wagons and firearms, the Boers inflicted heavy losses on the Zulu. The river reportedly ran red with blood, so Afrikaners remember it as **Blood River**.

This victory became a central story in Afrikaner history. The Boers felt their survival was proof of divine favor, a fulfillment of what some called a "covenant" with God. Afterward, the Boers established a foothold in Natal, setting up a short-lived Boer republic called **Republic of Natalia**. Tensions with the Zulu continued, but the balance of power in the region shifted.

---

4. Founding New Boer Communities

Republic of Natalia

After Blood River, some Trekkers settled near **Pietermaritzburg** and other parts of Natal, declaring themselves an independent republic. They laid out farms, built small towns, and tried to organize a government with elected officials, a council, and a legal system derived from Roman-Dutch law. However, the British had also taken an interest in Natal as a potential port area (Durban). By 1842, British forces moved in, eventually annexing Natal in 1843. The Boers who refused to live under British rule again moved further into the interior.

Transvaal and Orange Free State

Other Trekker groups ventured north of the Vaal River (into what came to be known as the **Transvaal** region) and across the Orange

River (the **Orange Free State** region). They negotiated or fought with local Sotho, Tswana, Pedi, and other communities. Over time, they declared small republics with names like **Potchefstroom** and **Zoutpansberg**. These smaller polities merged or changed alliances, eventually forming two more stable entities: the **South African Republic** (often called the Transvaal) and the **Orange Free State**.

These Boer republics were loosely structured at first, with a president, a volksraad (people's council or assembly), and a system of local commandos for defense. They recognized the Dutch Reformed Church as central to their community life. Land was allocated to settlers, though boundaries were often vague, and many indigenous communities disputed these claims. The stage was set for further conflicts that would shape the region in the late 19th century.

---

5. Interactions with Indigenous Communities

Mixed Forms of Coexistence

Not all Voortrekker relationships with African groups were hostile. In some places, Trekkers signed treaties or purchased land (though these arrangements were not always clear to local chiefs who had different ideas of land tenure). Some African communities saw the Boers as potential allies against rival groups. They traded cattle, goods, and labor, though the power imbalance often favored the well-armed settlers.

Missionaries sometimes acted as mediators, helping to draw up agreements or settle disputes. But, overall, the arrival of Trekkers disrupted established political systems in the interior. Kingdoms that once controlled large territories now faced new pressures or alliances. Many African farmers lost grazing areas or water sources to Boer claims, sparking future wars.

Labor and Servitude

Even though the Cape had abolished slavery, some Boer trekkers continued to rely on forms of forced or semi-forced labor. They might raid communities for cattle and captives, or use debt bondage where African families worked off obligations in farm labor. Children from conquered communities could be taken in as forced apprentices, an arrangement not officially called slavery but similar in practice. Over time, such labor relations became a major complaint of local African leaders and British missionaries. This tension contributed to further animosity and moral condemnation of the Boer settlements by outsiders.

---

6. Hardships on the Trek

Travel Dangers

Travel by ox wagon across rough terrain was not easy. Families faced swollen rivers, steep mountain passes, drought, and disease. Oxen could die from sickness like lung-sickness or tsetse-fly-borne diseases in certain regions. Food supplies ran low, leading to hunger and malnutrition. In winter, the nights were bitterly cold on the highveld; in summer, thunderstorms threatened wagon trains with lightning and hail.

Medical help was limited. Trek leaders or older women in the group might have knowledge of herbal remedies. Serious injuries or illnesses often proved fatal. Childbirth was risky on the road, with no settled homesteads or established midwives. Families had to bury loved ones in unmarked graves far from any churchyard, relying on faith and their traveling community for comfort.

Resilience and Adaptation

Despite these hardships, many families found ways to adapt. They learned how to repair wagons, shoe oxen, and sew new clothes from local materials. Some traded with African communities for sorghum, maize, or livestock. They adapted diets to include more game meat. Over time, they built temporary laagers where they grew small gardens or set up makeshift corrals for livestock. Their ability to move on short notice—wagons packed and commandos ready—became both a survival tactic and a defining characteristic of the Trekker lifestyle.

---

7. Cultural and Religious Identity

The "Covenant" Tradition

A recurring theme in Trekker narratives is the belief that God granted them success in battles like Blood River. According to some accounts, before the battle, the Boers made a "covenant" with God: if He granted them victory, they would remember the day and build a church in His honor. After winning decisively, they viewed themselves as a chosen people with a divine mission. While historical details of this vow vary, it became deeply ingrained in **Afrikaner** culture.

The date of the battle, December 16, turned into a sacred day among many Afrikaners, celebrated in later years as the **Day of the Vow** or the **Day of the Covenant**. This religious interpretation of historical events shaped a powerful group identity, reinforcing the idea that the Trekkers were forging a God-fearing nation in the wilderness.

Language and Traditions

Afrikaans was not yet fully formed as it is today, but the Dutch spoken by the Trekkers was evolving, influenced by contact with other languages like Malay, Portuguese creole, and African languages. Trekker families told stories around campfires of old

Dutch heroes, biblical sagas, and past conflicts with the British. Songs and prayers in Dutch Reformed style bound communities together. Even without official schools, children learned from elders to read the Bible in Dutch, or at least to recite prayers and psalms.

These traditions laid the groundwork for a distinct Afrikaner culture that developed further in the republics they founded. Over time, new generations called themselves **Afrikaners**, linking their identity to the African land they now inhabited and shaped.

---

8. British Responses and Annexations

Natal Annexation

When the Boers in Natal formed the Republic of Natalia, they hoped for independence. But the port of Durban was strategically important to the British. In 1842, British forces clashed with the Boers, capturing key positions. By 1843, Britain formally annexed Natal. Some Voortrekkers refused to accept this and left for the interior again, while others stayed and lived under British rule.

Orange River Sovereignty

Further inland, the British were also wary of letting new Boer states develop too freely. They claimed authority over lands between the Orange and Vaal Rivers (the area sometimes called the **Orange River Sovereignty**), partly to keep order in conflicts between Boers and local African groups. However, maintaining control over a large territory with limited troops proved difficult. After a few years, Britain agreed to recognize some measure of Boer independence in what became the **Orange Free State** (1854). A similar arrangement eventually formed in the Transvaal (1852), where Britain signed the Sand River Convention.

Thus, by the mid-1850s, two Boer republics existed officially—**Orange Free State** and **South African Republic (Transvaal)**—both recognized by Britain under certain conditions. This recognition did not end conflicts with African polities, nor did it prevent future tensions between the republics and the British Empire. But it solidified the political map, giving shape to a divided South Africa that would last well into the future.

9. Long-Term Consequences of the Great Trek

Shaping Political Divisions

The Great Trek deeply influenced the layout of southern Africa. It led to the creation of new Boer states in the interior, separate from the British-ruled Cape and Natal colonies. Each area followed its own path of governance, laws, and interactions with indigenous communities. Over time, these divides would contribute to a patchwork of colonial states—Cape Colony, Natal, Transvaal, and Orange Free State—each with its own identity and struggles.

Lasting Conflicts

The Great Trek ignited many wars on the frontier. African kingdoms, such as the Zulu, Swazi, Sotho, Pedi, and Tswana polities, fought to defend their lands against the encroaching Trekkers. Sometimes the Boers aligned with smaller chiefdoms or used divide-and-rule strategies. Large-scale battles, forced population movements, and shifting alliances changed the region's demographic and political landscape. These conflicts laid roots for future disputes, eventually drawing in the British again when diamonds and gold were discovered later in the century.

Cultural Legacy

For Afrikaner nationalism, the Great Trek became a central legend, symbolizing perseverance, faith, and the quest for freedom. Later generations memorialized leaders like Retief and Pretorius as heroes. Events like the Battle of Blood River were remembered in monuments, ceremonies, and school lessons. While the trek itself was not a single unified movement, it provided a shared heritage that shaped Afrikaner identity and ideology, especially during the late 19th and 20th centuries.

10. Life in the Boer Republics

Governance Structures

In the newly formed republics, political power lay with a **President** and a **Volksraad** (people's council), both chosen by landowning citizens—almost exclusively white males. The republics claimed to uphold Roman-Dutch law tempered by frontier traditions and Calvinist teachings. This system was simple, often underfunded, and reliant on local commandos for defense. Farmers lived far apart, connected loosely by wagon roads and occasional markets in small towns.

Economy and Society

Farming remained the backbone of these communities, mostly raising livestock (cattle, sheep) and growing some crops. Trade caravans occasionally reached coastal ports, exchanging ivory, skins, or other products for gunpowder, cloth, and manufactured goods. Wealth differences grew between those with large herds or successful farms and poorer settlers who struggled on less fertile land.

Labor systems in the republics often involved forms of indenture or coerced labor for Africans. Although formal slavery was illegal, in practice, many black families lived under harsh conditions on Boer farms. Churches offered spiritual guidance and tried to set moral standards, but conflict with indigenous groups remained frequent. Infrastructure like roads, schools, and medical facilities was limited, reflecting the frontier character of these republics.

CHAPTER 9

THE BOER REPUBLICs EMERGE

Introduction

After the Great Trek (discussed in Chapter 8), Dutch-speaking farmers known as **Voortrekkers** had moved far from the Cape Colony to escape British rule and create their own communities. Over time, these communities formed more solid structures, becoming the **Boer Republics**. Two main republics took shape: the **South African Republic** (often called the Transvaal) and the **Orange Free State**. These entities developed their own systems of government, laws, and social customs.

In this chapter, we will explore how the Boer Republics emerged from rough wagon camps to more organized states. We will look at how they governed themselves, how they interacted with neighboring African groups, and what life was like for families building new homes on the high plains of the interior. We will also examine the role of religion, the economy of farming and trade, and the conflicts that arose as these republics tried to remain separate from British influence. By the end of this chapter, you will have a good understanding of how the Boer Republics came into being, and why they mattered so much in South African history before the discovery of major mineral wealth.

1. Roots in the Great Trek

The story of the Boer Republics begins with the **Great Trek** of the 1830s and 1840s, when groups of Dutch-speaking colonists left the

Cape Colony to find new lands. These trekking groups—called **Voortrekkers**—were made up of families who wanted freedom from British taxes, laws, and the ban on slavery. They traveled in ox-drawn wagons, braving unknown territories and defending themselves against various dangers.

At first, each group was led by its own prominent individual (such as Andries Potgieter, Hendrik Potgieter, Piet Retief, or Andries Pretorius). They formed small camps called **laagers** for protection. Over time, these groups realized they needed better organization to handle issues like defense, disputes over farmland, and the arrangement of basic governance. This realization was the seed from which the Boer Republics eventually grew.

Early Attempts at Government

In the early trekking days, leadership was informal. A head of a group might be chosen for his military or organizational skill. Councils of men would gather around campfires to discuss treaties, punishments for crimes, and how to share grazing lands. Decisions were often based on old Dutch customs and biblical teachings because most Trekkers followed the Dutch Reformed faith very closely.

As the trekkers settled in different regions—north of the Vaal River, for instance—they needed a more stable form of government. Their families and livestock spread out across wide areas, leading to small farmland communities that still had to cooperate for common defense. Gradually, they began calling themselves **"Boers,"** meaning "farmers" in Dutch. The label captured their identity as rural, self-reliant people who worked the land.

2. Founding of the Transvaal (South African Republic)

Naming and Location

The word "Transvaal" means "across the Vaal River." The region got its name from its location north of the Vaal, one of the major rivers that separated it from the Cape Colony and from the Orange River area. As more Voortrekkers established farms in this area, they formed small settlements like **Potchefstroom**, **Zoutpansberg**, **Lydenburg**, and **Pretoria** (named later for Andries Pretorius).

Over time, these scattered areas tried to unite. They all saw themselves as Boers, but they had different local leaders and slight variations in how they managed communities. By the early 1850s, talks began about forming a single state. The **Sand River Convention** (1852) was a key milestone: the British recognized the independence of the Boers north of the Vaal River, effectively creating what became known as the **South African Republic** or simply the Transvaal Republic.

The Volksraad and Presidents

To manage public affairs, the Boers created a **Volksraad**, which means "people's council" in Dutch. This body was made up of elected representatives—generally land-owning, white, male citizens who were members of the Dutch Reformed Church. The Volksraad would pass laws, decide on taxes, and handle matters like treaties with African groups. Because of the rough frontier environment, many people carried weapons, so the government's power partly depended on the willingness of local commandos to back its decisions.

The head of state became the **President**. In early years, strong personalities rose to the top. For example, **M.W. Pretorius** (son of the well-known Andries Pretorius) served as a key figure in unifying different Boer areas. Presidents usually had to juggle many responsibilities: controlling internal disagreements, dealing with outside pressures, and making sure farmland was secure against raiders or rival claimants.

Legal System and Roman-Dutch Law

The Transvaal claimed to follow **Roman-Dutch law**, inherited from the Cape's early Dutch traditions. But in practice, the law on the frontier was sometimes enforced by local commandos or through local leaders known as **field cornets**, who had policing and administrative duties. Punishments could be severe, and the legal processes were not always as formal as in established states. Nonetheless, the Boers took pride in their legal heritage, seeing it as distinct from British common law.

Because many settlers lived far from towns, actual enforcement of laws could be patchy. People in remote homesteads often resolved disputes themselves, turning to the official courts only if there was a major conflict. This do-it-yourself approach to justice suited the frontier conditions but sometimes caused confusion over property rights, labor contracts, and the treatment of indigenous inhabitants.

---

3. Founding of the Orange Free State

Location Between Two Rivers

Another group of Voortrekkers made their homes between the **Orange River** and the **Vaal River**. This region became known as the **Orange River Sovereignty** when the British tried to assert control, hoping to reduce conflict between the Boers and local African chiefdoms. But the British soon found it costly and difficult to manage. Following some clashes and negotiations, the British withdrew in 1854 under the **Bloemfontein Convention**, recognizing the independence of the Boers in that area. Thus, the **Orange Free State** came into existence.

The name reflects the Orange River, which in turn was named by early Dutch explorers in honor of the Dutch royal family (the House of Orange). The new republic had its capital at **Bloemfontein**, a modest town that began as a simple trading center and frontier outpost. From here, an elected President and Volksraad tried to organize the state's affairs.

Government Structure and Politics

Similar to the Transvaal, the **Orange Free State** had a **Volksraad**, and voters were adult, white, male burghers, usually Dutch Reformed in religion. They elected a President who worked with an Executive Council. Early presidents included leaders like **J.P. Hoffman** and later **Sir John Henry Brand**, who tried to strengthen the state and maintain peaceful relations with neighbors. Brand, for example, served many years and was well respected for diplomacy.

Politically, the Orange Free State had fewer internal divisions than the Transvaal because it had a smaller population and fewer scattered settlements. It also had more consistent leadership at times, which helped it build a stable if modest government apparatus. Unlike the Transvaal, which was huge and had remote districts, the Orange Free State was somewhat easier to manage.

Dealing with Surrounding Groups

The Orange Free State shared borders with African communities such as the **Sotho** under **King Moshoeshoe I**, whose stronghold was at **Thaba Bosiu** in the Basotho Kingdom. Conflicts over land and cattle raids led to wars, especially in the 1850s and 1860s. Although not as famous worldwide as later Boer-British wars, these Sotho-Boer conflicts shaped life in the region and tested the new republic's military capacity.

In some treaties, land was ceded or disputed boundaries were drawn, but they often caused more confusion. The British, who still had interests in controlling southern Africa's overall stability, sometimes acted as arbitrators or stepped in with their own aims. Nonetheless, the Orange Free State managed to hold its own ground, forging an identity as a Boer republic that valued independence and wanted minimal interference from outsiders.

4. Society, Culture, and Religion in the Boer Republics

Daily Life on the Frontier

Life in the Boer Republics was generally rural and centered on farming. Families lived in simple homesteads, often built of mud bricks or stone, with thatched roofs. They kept livestock—cattle, sheep, goats—and farmed crops like maize (mielies), wheat, and vegetables if water was available. Water sources were crucial; many families settled near rivers or springs. Because the climate could be harsh, with hot summers and cold winters on the highveld, survival required practical skills and cooperation among neighbors.

Travel was mainly by **ox wagon** or **horseback**. Visits to towns might happen only once every few weeks or months, to buy supplies or attend church. Social gatherings were often linked to church events, weddings, or communal work parties. The isolation helped shape a culture that prized self-reliance, hospitality to visitors, and close family ties.

Role of the Dutch Reformed Church

Religion was at the heart of Boer culture. The **Dutch Reformed Church** was the most common denomination, continuing the tradition brought from the Cape. Pastors were in short supply, so they traveled great distances to conduct services in small, scattered congregations. Large gatherings for communion (nagmaal) sometimes turned into social events lasting several days.

The Bible was central in daily life, guiding moral views and family routines. Many families read from it daily, seeing themselves as chosen to uphold a Christian way of life in the interior of Africa. This strong faith also shaped views of other communities, including local African groups, with some Boers believing they had a biblical right to control land and labor.

Language: From Dutch to Early Afrikaans

While official documents were written in Dutch, the spoken language among Boers evolved into a distinct dialect that would later become **Afrikaans**. It was influenced by many sources, including local African languages, Malay from enslaved people who had once lived at the Cape, and older forms of Dutch. However, during the mid-1800s, people did not yet call this language "Afrikaans." They saw it as a simpler or "kitchen" form of Dutch, used mainly in everyday conversation. Over time, it grew into a recognized language.

---

5. Relations with African Communities

Complex Patchwork of Chiefdoms

The interior of southern Africa was not empty. Many African polities lived there, each with its own traditions, leaders, and territory. These included groups like the **Sotho**, **Tswana**, **Pedi**, **Ndebele**, **Swazi**, and smaller chiefdoms scattered across the highveld. The Boers' arrival created new tensions over land, cattle, and water sources.

Some African communities initially traded with the Boers, swapping cattle or ivory for guns, horses, or European goods. Others tried to keep them out. A few sought alliances with one Boer group against a neighboring African rival. This gave some Boers the chance to expand territory by intervening in local conflicts. But it also meant the Boer Republics often found themselves in a cycle of treaties, raids, and reprisals.

Wars and Dispossession

When peaceful trade gave way to conflict, Boer commandos (armed farmers) would gather to protect their livestock or claim territory. They had firearms and horses, which often gave them an edge in battle. However, certain African kingdoms, such as the **Pedi** and **Sotho**, mounted fierce resistance, using their own strategic positions and warrior traditions.

Over time, many African communities lost large portions of their land. Some were forced to become laborers on Boer farms or move to more remote areas. Others tried to bargain for peace or accept partial agreements that recognized some parts of their original territories. These arrangements were not always respected by the Boers or by individual settlers who wanted more farmland. Thus, the Boer Republics saw ongoing friction on nearly every border.

Labor Practices

Although formal slavery had ended at the Cape, labor practices in the republics still often involved forms of servitude or forced labor. Some Boers captured local people during conflicts, assigning them as **apprentices** or **inboekselings** (indentured children) under conditions close to slavery. Missionaries from Europe or the Cape criticized these practices, leading to further conflict between the Boer states and outside religious or humanitarian groups.

Boer farmers generally believed they needed African labor to manage large herds and farms. Wages were sometimes low or paid in goods rather than cash. Workers' freedom of movement could be limited by "passes," making it hard for them to leave or seek better opportunities. This dynamic set the stage for future tensions about labor rights and racial inequality, long before the modern era.

---

6. Economy of the Boer Republics

Farming and Ranching

Most Boers engaged in **pastoral farming**, raising cattle, sheep, and goats for meat, milk, and wool. Crops like maize, wheat, and vegetables supplied food for families, with any surplus sold in local towns. Wool became important for trade, especially once global demand for wool cloth rose. Some farmers did well, exporting wool through long wagon routes to the Cape or Natal ports.

Boers also hunted wildlife, such as antelope, to supplement their diet or trade skins and ivory. However, as populations grew, wild game declined. This caused some Boers to move again to find fresh pasture or hunting grounds. The constant movement made stable infrastructure—like roads and towns—harder to develop.

Trade and Transport

Because these republics were landlocked, they relied on wagons to carry goods to ports controlled by the British—mainly in Natal or the Cape Colony. The journey was slow and could be dangerous. Flooded rivers, banditry, or broken wheels caused delays. Transport riders who specialized in carrying goods (sometimes known as **transport riders** or **smouse**) created a small but vital trade network. They brought in gunpowder, fabrics, coffee, sugar, and manufactured items, exchanging them for farm produce or livestock.

A few small towns like **Potchefstroom**, **Pietersburg**, **Bloemfontein**, and **Winburg** emerged as market centers where wagon trains stopped. Blacksmiths, wheelwrights, and general shops sprang up, serving both Boers and local African communities. Still, the scale of trade was modest, and the overall economy of the republics stayed quite simple until the discovery of diamonds and gold in later years.

Monetary and Banking Practices

At first, many transactions used barter—trading goods directly. Gradually, British coinage from the Cape or foreign coins entered circulation, but there was never a strong local currency in the early days of the republics. Attempts to start banks or issue paper money ran into challenges, partly because people distrusted anything but metal coins or direct goods exchange. The small scale of business, combined with periodic conflicts, made stable banking difficult.

---

7. British Reaction and Early Pressures

Diplomatic Maneuvers

While the Boers saw themselves as independent, Britain kept an eye on the region. It worried that the Boer Republics might cause trouble with African communities, thus destabilizing borders near British colonies. Also, British officials did not want any other European power—like Portugal or Germany—to gain influence there. Therefore, the British occasionally meddled or demanded that the Boers respect boundaries, sign treaties, or halt certain conflicts.

Tensions rose whenever the republics tried to expand or when British missionaries complained about abuses of African populations in Boer areas. Sometimes, British officials threatened intervention, and the Boer governments had to tread carefully. They did not want to be swallowed up by the British Empire, but they also needed to maintain trade links for basic supplies.

Annexation Fears

Throughout the mid-1800s, there were rumors that Britain might annex the Boer lands outright. Indeed, Britain had tried to hold the Orange River Sovereignty once before. Only financial concerns and the complexity of frontier rule had made them give it up. Still, the fear of British annexation never vanished. Boer leaders tried to show Britain that they could manage their own affairs responsibly, though trust between them remained low.

When friction arose along the frontiers—like the conflicts with Basotho or other African polities—Britain sometimes stepped in as a mediator. If the dispute escalated, the Boers worried it could open a path for Britain to reoccupy or enforce new conditions. These uneasy dynamics continued until events in the 1870s and beyond shifted the balance yet again. But that is a future topic we will touch on in later chapters.

---

8. Internal Challenges and Rivalries

Divisions Among Boers

Not all Boers agreed on how to run the republics. Some wanted a centralized authority with a strong presidency. Others preferred local independence, letting each district manage itself. Personal rivalries between leaders like Andries Pretorius, M.W. Pretorius, and others led to multiple power struggles. This was especially true in the Transvaal, which was large and sparsely populated, making it hard for any one faction to control the entire region.

In addition, the local commandos sometimes acted independently, creating tension if they fought African communities without official permission. The government had to balance the desire to protect settlers with the risk of sparking bigger wars. These internal strains sometimes made the republics unstable, with short-lived governments or contested elections.

Financial Problems

Another big challenge was money. Running even a small republic required funds for administration, salaries of officials, public roads, and defense. But the Boers, mostly small-scale farmers, disliked paying taxes. Many felt that as free people living off the land, they should not owe large sums to any government. Consequently, the treasuries of the Transvaal and Orange Free State stayed lean, limiting the ability to build schools, roads, or advanced defenses.

Some leaders tried new taxes on imported goods, but this angered local merchants and transport riders. Efforts to create a stable currency also faced resistance. As a result, the state remained weak in many aspects, leaning heavily on the readiness of ordinary Boers to form commandos or volunteer for tasks like building a courthouse or a church.

---

9. Everyday Life and Family Structures

Homestead and Gender Roles

Within Boer families, the father was typically seen as head of the household, responsible for major decisions and religious guidance. Women, however, played key roles in running daily life, caring for children, cooking, tending gardens, and even helping with farm tasks when needed. Because the environment was harsh, everyone had to pitch in. Women also provided moral support during conflicts or long journeys, passing on their skills and knowledge to children.

Children grew up learning practical skills from a young age. Boys handled livestock, practiced shooting, and learned to ride horses.

Girls helped with cooking, sewing, and caring for younger siblings. Formal schooling was irregular in many areas, though families who valued education might hire a traveling tutor or send children to a mission school if one was nearby. However, for many, reading and writing skills were taught at home using the Bible as a text.

Celebrations and Community Events

Despite the hardships, the Boer communities had joyful moments. Weddings were large gatherings, often lasting several days. Relatives traveled by wagon from far-off farms, bringing food and gifts. There would be dancing, singing of psalms, and big meals. The same happened at **nagmaal** (communion) services in the local church, which also served as a social event where people swapped news, formed friendships, or settled disputes.

Seasonal activities included harvest times and cattle roundups. Harvest celebrations, if the rains had been good, could be festive. Some farmers took pride in breeding strong horses or high-quality livestock. Indeed, a man's status rose if he had well-kept herds and a tidy homestead. Hospitality was important: travelers passing by could often expect a meal and a place to stay, given the custom of helping strangers in a land where inns were scarce.

---

10. Approaching a New Era

Tensions Beneath the Surface

By the late 1850s and 1860s, the Boer Republics were established but faced ongoing challenges. Conflicts with African neighbors continued to flare up. Britain remained cautious about their independence. Internal divisions over leadership persisted, and the economy struggled without major industries or well-developed trade routes.

No one at the time knew that the entire region would soon be transformed by the discovery of **diamonds** (around Kimberley in the 1860s and 1870s) and later **gold** (on the Witwatersrand in the 1880s). Those events would bring new wealth, new conflicts, and a major shift in power dynamics. For now, the Boer Republics were modest farming states, proud of their freedom from Britain but aware that the world outside might not always respect their independence.

Significance of the Boer Republics

The emergence of the Transvaal and Orange Free State is key to understanding South African history. These republics showed the Boers' determination to live by their own laws, language, and religion. They shaped a strong sense of **Afrikaner** identity, rooted in the memories of the Great Trek and the faith-driven worldview that saw them as chosen people in a land they believed was theirs to tame.

As we move to the next chapter, the discovery of minerals will change the path of these republics, leading to new challenges and transformations. The conflicts that arise from the Mineral Revolution will cast a long shadow, eventually drawing both the Boer states and Britain into deeper struggles. But for now, the republics stand as proud and independent, albeit fragile, polities on the high plains of southern Africa.

CHAPTER 10

DIAMONDS, GOLD, AND THE MINERAL REVOLUTION

Introduction

South Africa's interior remained relatively quiet and agrarian during the early days of the Boer Republics. Farming communities dotted the landscape, reliant on ox-wagon travel, subsistence crops, and small-scale trade. But this steady rhythm was about to change dramatically. In the late 1860s and early 1870s, **diamonds** were discovered near the confluence of the Vaal and Orange Rivers—an event that brought thousands of prospectors seeking fortune. Soon after, the discovery of **gold** on the Witwatersrand in the 1880s transformed the region even more, ushering in the **Mineral Revolution**.

This chapter explores how diamonds and gold were found, the rush of fortune-seekers, and the formation of large mining towns like **Kimberley** and **Johannesburg**. We will see how the Mineral Revolution greatly affected the local economy, social structures, labor systems, and power relations. It turned southern Africa into a hot spot for international investment, intensified conflicts between the Boer Republics and the British Empire, and led to major social changes for African communities forced into labor. By the end of this chapter, you will understand why the discovery of diamonds and gold stands as a turning point that reshaped the whole course of South Africa's history—though we will still stop short of modern times, focusing on the immediate decades of transformation.

1. Early Diamond Discoveries

Hints and Rumors

Long before an official diamond rush, there were rumors of shiny stones found along riverbanks in southern Africa. In the late 1860s, travelers and traders along the **Vaal River** began to show interest in pebbles that turned out to be diamonds. A famous early find was the **Eureka Diamond** (1866 or 1867), reportedly picked up by a child on a farm near the Orange River. This stone was eventually recognized as a diamond of about 21 carats.

Word spread quickly, and soon fortune-hunters—mostly from the Cape Colony, Britain, Europe, and even America—poured into the region. At the time, these lands were contested. Some farms lay in the northern Cape, others in what the Boer Republics claimed, and others in the area claimed by African groups like the **Griqua** or the **Tlhaping**. The boundaries were not always clear. This confusion set the stage for disputes over diamond fields and who actually owned them.

Rush to the Fields

By the early 1870s, a full-fledged diamond rush was underway. Prospectors used picks, shovels, and primitive sieves to search for stones in river gravels and in the dry diggings around what became **Kimberley** (initially called New Rush). Men lived in tents or makeshift shacks, forming chaotic camps. The noise, dust, and excitement gave the diamond fields a wild frontier spirit.

As more diamonds were found, thousands of people arrived. Small claims changed hands quickly, as some lucky diggers struck it rich while others gave up. The Cape government tried to extend its control over the region, claiming that the diamond fields fell under British authority. Meanwhile, the Boer Republics disputed these claims, insisting that certain areas belonged to them. Conflicts emerged, and eventually, Britain used the diamond disputes as part of its strategy to reassert power in the interior.

---

2. Kimberley and the Organization of Diamond Mining

Birth of Kimberley

The biggest diamond deposits were around four "dry diggings" that merged into a single massive mining area. This settlement took on the name **Kimberley**, after Lord Kimberley, a British Colonial Secretary. Kimberley grew rapidly into a bustling town filled with shops, saloons, and suppliers catering to miners. Wooden and corrugated iron structures sprang up, with little planning. Dirt roads turned to mud in rainy seasons, and sanitation was poor.

However, the wealth drawn from diamonds meant that some individuals made fortunes. Over time, local authorities tried to impose order, selling or leasing plots of land for digging. Roads were laid out more systematically, and a rudimentary municipal system formed. Kimberley soon became the largest city in the interior, overshadowing older Boer towns in terms of population and economic clout.

New Mining Methods

Initially, each claim was small, and miners worked with picks and spades, digging by hand or with a partner. If a vein of diamond-bearing rock extended beyond one claim, it was complicated to follow. Flooding from underground water and cave-ins made deep digging dangerous. Over time, bigger operators bought out smaller claims, introducing machinery like steam-powered pumps and hoists.

Two major companies rose to dominance in Kimberley's diamond fields: those led by **Cecil Rhodes** and **Barney Barnato**, both from modest British backgrounds. By buying claims from small diggers who ran out of money, these men built large syndicates. Eventually, Rhodes and Barnato merged, creating **De Beers Consolidated Mines** in 1888. This monopoly could control diamond supply, stabilize prices, and influence colonial politics.

Impact on Boer Republics and Local Communities

The diamond fields lay in a zone the British soon proclaimed as **Griqualand West**, an area annexed to the Cape Colony. The **Orange Free State** had a competing claim. After legal battles and arbitration, the British side largely prevailed, leaving the Orange Free State bitter but receiving some financial compensation. The Transvaal also gained little from diamonds directly, as most fields fell outside its borders, although some Transvaal farmers profited by supplying goods to the fields.

African workers arrived in Kimberley too, seeking wages. But working conditions were harsh. Mine owners saw that controlling labor was key to making profits. They introduced pass systems, fenced compounds, and strict rules to prevent diamond theft. These measures set patterns for controlling black labor that would be refined during the later **gold** era. Already, the seeds of a racially divided labor system were being planted, with African mine workers subject to curfews, searches, and limited mobility.

---

3. Discovery of Gold on the Witwatersrand

Early Gold Finds in the Eastern Transvaal

Before the big discovery on the **Witwatersrand**, gold had been found in the eastern Transvaal (near places like Pilgrim's Rest and

Barberton) in the 1870s. These small gold rushes caused some excitement but did not transform the economy in the same way diamonds did in Kimberley. The reefs were limited, and the technology to extract deep gold was not advanced enough.

Still, these smaller finds gave the Transvaal government hope. If a bigger gold deposit turned up, the republic might gain wealth to strengthen its independence and build roads, railways, or better administrative systems. Some prospectors continued searching other parts of the Transvaal, especially the ridge known as the **Witwatersrand**, near present-day Johannesburg.

The Witwatersrand Bonanza (1886)

In 1886, the real mother lode was discovered. Prospectors found extensive **reef gold** deposits on the Witwatersrand ("ridge of white waters"). Unlike alluvial gold from rivers, this gold was trapped in ancient conglomerate rock called **banket**. Extracting it required deep-level mining, crushing the rock, and using chemical processes (like mercury or cyanide) to separate the gold. This technology was expensive but promised huge returns if done on a large scale.

A frenzy erupted. People poured into the area from across southern Africa and abroad. A tent city sprang up, eventually becoming **Johannesburg**—named after officials Johannes Joubert or Johannes Rissik (accounts vary). Johannesburg expanded at a breakneck pace, with wooden shacks, shops, saloons, and banks. Within a few years, it became the biggest city in southern Africa, surpassing even Kimberley.

---

4. The Mineral Revolution Takes Shape

Economic Shift

With diamond and gold mining booming, the economy of the region changed from being mostly rural and agricultural to one driven by

extractive industry. Large mining companies emerged, requiring huge investments. British and European financiers were eager to put money into these ventures, hoping for big profits. These companies introduced modern technology: drills, pumps, dynamite, and refining facilities.

Railways soon became essential. The Cape Colony extended tracks to Kimberley and, later, lines were built into the Transvaal to reach the gold fields. The Orange Free State also allowed rail lines to cross its territory in return for certain fees. Instead of months by ox wagon, supplies and people could now move in days or hours by train. This was part of the **Mineral Revolution**: a total reshaping of transportation, finance, and labor.

Rise of Urban Centers

Kimberley provided a model for how a mining town could grow and transform into a city. Johannesburg followed suit but at an even faster pace. The need to house thousands of miners, shopkeepers, bankers, and laborers meant that new residential districts appeared. High demand for building materials and food products spurred further business opportunities. Immigrants from Britain, the rest of Europe, North America, Australia, and other places arrived, bringing new skills and ideas.

Tension also grew, because these big cities stood in the middle of what had been **Boer territory**. The Transvaal government found itself hosting a large population of **uitlanders** (foreigners), many of them English-speaking. These newcomers demanded roads, sanitation, policing, and political rights—services the small Boer administration was unprepared to provide effectively. Conflicts emerged about voting rights and taxes, sowing seeds of future discord.

5. Labor Systems and Racial Controls

Compound System in Kimberley

Mine owners in Kimberley developed the **compound system** to control labor and reduce theft. African workers lived in enclosed barracks near the mines. They signed contracts for a fixed period. Inside these compounds, workers were subject to searches, had limited freedom to leave, and were separated from their families. The companies believed that restricting movement would minimize illicit diamond dealing and keep wages low.

Although the compound system was harsh, many African men took these jobs out of economic necessity. Rural areas offered few opportunities beyond subsistence farming, and colonial expansion often disrupted traditional livelihoods. Wages from the mines could be sent home to pay taxes (demanded by colonial governments) or buy goods. This new migrant labor pattern—men leaving families behind to work in faraway mines—became a hallmark of the southern African economy.

Migrant Labor for Gold Mines

Gold mining on the Witwatersrand expanded these labor practices even more. Deep-level mining required many unskilled workers to do tough, dangerous tasks underground. White miners typically held supervisory or skilled positions, earning higher wages. African workers, grouped by ethnic or regional background, performed the hardest labor. Their living conditions were crowded, with minimal health facilities.

Mine owners often worked together to keep wages low, forming **chambers of mines** that set standard pay rates and labor policies. The state supported these arrangements, seeing them as part of economic progress. Over time, the system of dividing workers by race and paying Africans significantly less became well entrenched. It also extended to other parts of society, with pass laws restricting African movement and housing discrimination. While we are still not focusing on modern times, the roots of later segregation policies were clearly planted during this Mineral Revolution era.

6. Influence on the Boer Republics and British Ambitions

Wealth in the Transvaal

The sudden wealth from gold put the **South African Republic (Transvaal)** in a strange position. On one hand, tax revenues soared, and new businesses appeared. The government began modernizing roads, telegraphs, and public buildings in **Pretoria**, the capital. On the other hand, the population of foreigners in Johannesburg skyrocketed. Many were English speakers who resented Boer laws, found them backward, and wanted the right to vote in the republic's elections.

President **Paul Kruger** led the Transvaal at this time. He tried to balance the Boer tradition of independence with the practical needs of a booming gold economy. Kruger increased tariffs and implemented laws that some uitlanders viewed as hostile or unfair (for instance, long waiting periods before foreigners could gain citizenship). This friction grew into a major point of tension between the Transvaal government and British interests.

Britain's Renewed Interest

Britain, seeing the vast wealth in gold, wanted to ensure that the region did not become a rival power. British politicians, imperial promoters like **Cecil Rhodes**, and investors all aimed to bring the Transvaal more firmly under British influence. They complained about the treatment of British subjects (the uitlanders) and alleged that the Transvaal leadership was corrupt or incompetent.

Already, Britain had seized control of the Transvaal once before, in 1877, citing mismanagement and conflict with local African groups. Boers rebelled, leading to the **First Anglo-Boer War** (1880–1881), which ended with a Boer victory at the Battle of Majuba Hill and a restoration of limited Transvaal independence under British suzerainty. With the discovery of gold, Britain's desire to control the Transvaal resurged. This situation foreshadowed more severe conflicts that would erupt later in the Anglo-Boer Wars (though we will handle those in a future chapter).

---

7. Effects on African Kingdoms and Communities

Loss of Autonomy

For African societies that had remained somewhat independent, the Mineral Revolution drastically changed power dynamics. Britain and the Boer republics, enriched by mining taxes and armed with better weapons, expanded their territories. African kingdoms such as those led by the **Pedi** or **Swazi** faced renewed pressure to submit or sign treaties that limited their sovereignty. Some were eventually annexed into neighboring colonies or republics.

This expansion often involved forced labor or heavy tribute, as well as new taxes that obliged African men to seek wage work in mines or on white-owned farms. Land once controlled by African communities fell into the hands of colonial or Boer authorities, who either sold it to white settlers or allocated it to large mining interests. In effect, the Mineral Revolution accelerated the dispossession of African peoples from their traditional lands.

Growing Migrant Labor Network

As the mines demanded more and more workers, a **regional migrant labor network** formed, reaching beyond the immediate borders of the Boer states or the Cape. Men from present-day Botswana, Lesotho, Mozambique, Zambia, Zimbabwe, and Malawi traveled (or were recruited) to work in the diamond and gold mines. This created widespread social changes: villages were missing many adult men for months or years at a time, families became dependent on cash wages, and cultural practices adapted to new economic realities.

Although some men returned home with money or purchased livestock, others stayed in the mining towns or renewed contracts, losing close ties to their home communities. The movement of so many people also spread diseases, adding another dimension to the changes brought by mining. Thus, the entire region of southern Africa began integrating into a single economic system centered on the mines.

8. Technological and Infrastructure Developments

Railways, Roads, and Telegraphs

Mining required fast, reliable transport of machinery, timber for shoring up shafts, and daily essentials for a large workforce. The British Cape Colony, guided by leaders like Cecil Rhodes (who became Prime Minister of the Cape in 1890), invested heavily in **railways** heading north toward Kimberley and then crossing into the interior. Soon, lines reached the outskirts of the Transvaal, and eventually, Pretoria and Johannesburg themselves.

The **Orange Free State** also allowed rail construction to connect Bloemfontein and other centers to the Cape lines. Although the Boers had been suspicious of foreign influence, they realized that railways could boost trade and bring them revenue from transit fees. Telegraph lines accompanied the tracks, allowing rapid communication. This web of transport and communication linked the far corners of southern Africa, tying once-isolated Boer republics into the global economy.

Urban Services and Public Works

Large municipalities like Kimberley and Johannesburg introduced **waterworks**, **electric lighting** (in the 1890s), and better roads or sewer systems—though improvements often lagged behind the booming population. Government agencies or private companies built these utilities, sometimes charging high fees. Many poor residents lived in slums or squatter camps without basic services.

Still, the arrival of such infrastructure was a leap beyond the simple, rural lifestyle that had prevailed. Even some Boer towns in the Transvaal began paving streets, installing telephones, and opening public libraries, reflecting the sudden influx of wealth. These urban developments stood in contrast to neglected rural districts, deepening divisions within both the Transvaal and the Orange Free State.

9. Social and Cultural Changes

Multicultural Towns

Mining centers became **cultural melting pots**. English soon dominated business and administration, but Dutch-speaking Boers also held positions of authority—at least in the Transvaal. Skilled white immigrants arrived from Britain, Germany, the United States, Australia, and elsewhere, bringing various languages and customs. Black African workers from many ethnic groups mixed in the compounds, each community striving to maintain cultural practices far from home.

Saloons, music halls, and theaters served the needs of wealthier individuals. Churches and missionary societies tried to provide moral and spiritual guidance. Newspapers sprang up, published in English, Dutch, and sometimes other languages, sharing news of new finds, politics, and local gossip. While some fortunes were made almost overnight, others fell into debt or lost everything gambling on claims that turned out to be worthless.

Tensions and Unequal Treatment

The new society was far from equal. White miners earned much higher wages than black laborers, who were restricted to manual tasks. They lived in separate neighborhoods, often with better facilities. Laws and social customs enforced racial segregation in public spaces. Meanwhile, black workers were expected to accept pass laws and the compound system, limiting their freedom.

Gender ratios were skewed in mining towns—most workers were men, leading to social problems like prostitution, alcohol abuse, and occasional violence. Women who came to the diggings (both white and black) found some opportunities for business—like running boarding houses or small shops—but faced dangers in rough, male-dominated environments. Over time, local governments introduced policing and regulations, but corruption and favoritism were common.

10. Setting the Stage for Conflict

Shifting Power Balance

By the late 1880s and 1890s, the **South African Republic (Transvaal)** had become one of the richest spots on earth due to gold. British interests, including Cecil Rhodes and the Chamber of Mines in Johannesburg, wielded enormous influence. The Orange Free State, less directly affected by gold but still close to the trade routes, also changed as railways and commerce increased. Cape Colony, under British rule, grew more confident and wealthier through taxes on exports and transport.

This shift in power had major implications. Britain saw the Boer republics as obstacles to a grander scheme of unifying southern Africa under the British flag. Boer leaders, especially President Paul Kruger, aimed to keep their independence and maintain control over the wealth generated by gold. Tensions over uitlander rights, trade policies, and political control mounted, as each side realized that whoever controlled the gold fields would have a tremendous advantage.

A Ticking Time Bomb

Many observers saw that armed conflict was likely if no compromise could be found. Britain had the world's most powerful navy, but the Boer republics had many determined, armed citizens well-versed in commando tactics. The stage was thus set for the **Anglo-Boer Wars** (also called the South African Wars), which would erupt at the end of the 19th century. But we will explore that more deeply in later chapters.

For now, it is enough to recognize that the **Mineral Revolution**—sparked by diamonds and gold—transformed South Africa from a scattering of agrarian communities into a globally important center of mining. It revolutionized transport, introduced new labor systems, and gave the Boer Republics a burst of wealth that alarmed the British. At the same time, it made life harder for many African communities who lost land or were pressed into harsh labor. Society became more complex, more unequal, and more connected to the global economy than ever before.

Conclusion of Chapter 10

The discovery of **diamonds** in the 1860s and **gold** in the 1880s transformed South Africa in ways few could have imagined. What started as a frontier backwater became a magnet for international fortune-seekers. Towns like **Kimberley** and **Johannesburg** rose almost overnight, powered by the scramble for minerals. The **Mineral Revolution** modernized transportation and finance, but it also brought new forms of labor control and segregation.

For the Boer Republics—once sleepy farming territories—mining riches brought both opportunity and peril. They gained revenue and an influx of people, but also faced mounting pressure from Britain and foreign residents demanding rights. African communities, meanwhile, saw traditional lands taken and were pushed into migrant labor systems. By the end of the 19th century, the region was on a collision course toward greater conflicts, which we will explore in future chapters. But for now, we mark this period as the turning point that pulled South Africa into a new era, shaped by the power and profit of mineral wealth.

CHAPTER 11

CONFLICTS AND THE ANGLO-ZULU WARS

Introduction

By the mid-to-late 1800s, southern Africa was a region of shifting alliances and rising tensions. The discovery of diamonds (and later gold) brought new wealth, but also stirred competition among the Cape Colony, the Boer republics, and the British government. In addition, there were still powerful African kingdoms, especially the **Zulu**, who had kept much of their independence and military strength. The clash between the Zulu kingdom and the British—commonly called the **Anglo-Zulu War** of 1879—became one of the most famous conflicts in South African history.

In this chapter, we will look at the background that led to the Anglo-Zulu Wars, the nature of the Zulu kingdom, and the ways British and colonial authorities tried to expand their power. We will examine key battles like **Isandlwana** and **Rorke's Drift**, exploring how the Zulu warriors initially shocked the British with their fighting skills. Finally, we will see how the war ended, what happened to the Zulu kingdom, and why these events shaped future conflicts in the region.

1. The Rise of the Zulu Kingdom

Shaka and Zulu Expansion

The **Zulu** emerged as a formidable kingdom in the early 19th century, largely due to the leadership of **King Shaka Zulu** (reigning around 1816–1828). Shaka reorganized the Zulu military, introduced new tactics (such as the **"horns of the buffalo"** formation), and trained his warriors to fight as a cohesive force. He also enforced strict discipline and loyalty within the Zulu nation. Under his rule, the kingdom grew by absorbing or conquering neighboring chiefdoms, creating a powerful state in southeastern Africa.

After Shaka's death, other rulers like **Dingane** and **Mpande** continued to expand or defend the Zulu territory. By the time the 1870s arrived, the Zulu kingdom still covered a large area north of the Thukela (Tugela) River in what is now KwaZulu-Natal. Its people were mostly farmers and herders, living in homesteads (amakhaya) spread across rolling hills. Yet they remained unified under a central monarchy, which commanded thousands of well-trained warriors (impi).

Relations with the British and Boers

As we have seen in previous chapters, the **Boers** (Dutch-speaking farmers) moved into the Natal region during the Great Trek of the 1830s. Conflicts arose—most famously, the killing of Piet Retief and his delegation by King Dingane, and the subsequent Battle of Blood River in 1838. Eventually, the British took control of **Natal** in the 1840s. The Zulu kingdom still remained independent to the north, but its leaders kept a wary eye on the British presence.

In these years, certain missionaries and traders ventured into Zulu territory. Some Zulu kings tolerated or even welcomed them if they brought useful goods. However, the Zulu monarchy guarded its sovereignty. By the 1870s, an ambitious British official named **Sir Henry Bartle Frere**, High Commissioner for the British colonies in southern Africa, wanted to confederate the region under British authority. He saw the independent Zulu kingdom as an obstacle. Meanwhile, within the Zulu kingdom, King **Cetshwayo** had taken the throne (1873). He continued the military traditions of his ancestors, causing British fears that the Zulu might threaten Natal or hamper further colonial expansion.

2. Escalating Tensions in the 1870s

Bartle Frere's Confederation Plan

Britain, fresh from securing diamond fields in Griqualand West and still dealing with disputes in the Transvaal, wanted a unified policy across southern Africa. Sir Bartle Frere believed that merging all local states—Cape Colony, Natal, the Transvaal (which the British had annexed in 1877), the Orange Free State (still independent), and African kingdoms—under British rule would create stability. However, the Zulu kingdom stood out as a powerful, independent state right next to the British colony of Natal. Frere saw the Zulu's strong military as both a danger and a reason to intervene.

The British also had paternalistic ideas about "civilizing" African societies. In official letters and speeches, colonial officials often portrayed the Zulu kingdom as harshly ruled by a warrior class. They argued that the Zulu monarchy threatened peace. Some such claims were exaggerated or based on biased reports. Yet they served as a justification for British interference. By late 1878, Frere was determined to force the Zulu into submission or accept British demands that would weaken King Cetshwayo's power.

The Border Dispute and British Ultimatum

One spark for the conflict was a **border dispute** along the boundary between Natal and Zululand. Certain pieces of land, especially in the disputed territory near the Thukela (Tugela) and Buffalo rivers, were claimed by Boer settlers (before the British annexation) and also by the Zulu. A commission was set up to settle the dispute, and it actually decided in favor of the Zulu claims. Frere, however, tried to use the commission's findings to impose harsh terms on King Cetshwayo.

In December 1878, Frere issued an **ultimatum** to the Zulu, demanding they disband their military system, allow British control of certain internal matters, and accept a British resident in their kingdom. King Cetshwayo could never agree to such demands without losing his authority. By January 1879, when the ultimatum expired, British forces were already massing on the border, waiting to invade Zululand.

---

3. The Outbreak of War: January 1879

British Invasion Force

British army units, along with colonial volunteers, crossed the Buffalo River into Zululand in early January 1879. The commander-in-chief was **Lord Chelmsford**. He split his forces into columns, planning a three-pronged invasion to surround the Zulu capital (the royal homestead near Ulundi) and force King Cetshwayo to surrender. The British soldiers were confident, armed with modern rifles and artillery. Many believed the war would be quick.

However, they underestimated the Zulu. The Zulu warriors, though lacking firearms of the same quality, had discipline, knowledge of the terrain, and large numbers. They could march long distances and were skilled at using **assegais** (short stabbing spears), cowhide shields, and older muskets or rifles captured in earlier conflicts.

The Battle of Isandlwana (January 22, 1879)

One of the most striking events happened very early in the war: the **Battle of Isandlwana**. A large portion of Lord Chelmsford's central column encamped near a distinctive hill called Isandlwana. They did not fortify their position well, expecting no major Zulu attack. But on January 22, a Zulu army of around 20,000 warriors surprised the camp. The British soldiers were spread out and unprepared. Despite superior weapons, they were overwhelmed by the Zulu's rapid assault and encirclement tactics.

The result was a **shocking British defeat**. Over 1,300 British and colonial troops were killed, and the Zulu captured much equipment and ammunition. Isandlwana remains one of the biggest upsets in colonial warfare, proving that the Zulu could defeat a well-armed imperial force in open battle if they caught them off-guard. News of the defeat caused panic in Natal and alarm in Britain. Yet, it also hardened the British resolve to crush the Zulu kingdom.

Rorke's Drift (January 22-23, 1879)

On the same day, a smaller Zulu force of about 3,000 warriors attacked a British supply station at **Rorke's Drift**, a trading post converted into a temporary hospital and storehouse. Roughly 150 British defenders (including some wounded men) held off the Zulu assault through the night. They built barricades with mealie bags and biscuit boxes. In fierce hand-to-hand and rifle fighting, the defenders managed to repel waves of attackers. Eventually, the Zulu withdrew.

The battle of Rorke's Drift became famous in Britain, celebrated as a heroic stand that offset the disaster at Isandlwana. Several defenders were awarded the Victoria Cross for bravery. However, from the Zulu perspective, Rorke's Drift was a minor engagement compared to the huge victory at Isandlwana. Still, these two battles together defined the early stage of the Anglo-Zulu War—showing both the Zulu kingdom's fighting power and the British army's determination to retaliate.

---

4. British Reinforcements and the Shift in Momentum

Reacting to Isandlwana

The British, stunned by the Isandlwana loss, rushed reinforcements to Natal. More troops arrived by sea from Britain, along with better supply lines. Lord Chelmsford reorganized his columns, moving cautiously into Zululand in the following months. In April and May, the British carried out smaller engagements, capturing or destroying Zulu homesteads. Some local Zulu chiefs, worried about British firepower, began to submit or remain neutral.

Cetshwayo tried to negotiate, sending messages that he wanted peace if the British withdrew. However, British authorities, especially

Frere and Chelmsford, insisted on unconditional surrender. They believed they had to break the Zulu military system once and for all. Meanwhile, the British press and public demanded a swift victory to avenge their losses.

Further Battles

There were additional clashes, such as the battles of **Hlobane** and **Kambula** in March 1879. At **Hlobane**, the Zulu inflicted heavy losses on a small British raiding force. But the next day at **Kambula**, the British held strong defensive positions and beat back a large Zulu attack, inflicting significant casualties. These back-and-forth battles proved that while the Zulu were courageous and skilled, modern rifles and artillery could tip the scales if the British were prepared.

As the British columns pushed deeper, they burned crops and destroyed homesteads, reducing Zulu resources. Some groups of Zulu warriors became demoralized or starved. Disease also spread. King Cetshwayo tried to rally his forces, but the kingdom was under severe strain.

---

5. The Final Defeat of the Zulu (July 1879)

The Battle of Ulundi

Lord Chelmsford set his sights on **Ulundi**, the royal Zulu capital. In early July 1879, a reinforced British column marched there. On July 4, they met the main Zulu army near the White Umfolozi River. Learning from past mistakes, the British formed a tight infantry square, protected by cavalry on the flanks and supported by artillery and Gatling guns. When the Zulu attacked, they faced a hail of bullets and shells. Unable to break the formation, they suffered heavy losses.

This **Battle of Ulundi** spelled doom for King Cetshwayo's rule. The British burned the royal homestead, and Zulu resistance collapsed. Although some Zulu forces continued small-scale fighting, the monarchy had lost its core. Cetshwayo fled but was captured a few weeks later. The British victory was assured.

Aftermath for Cetshwayo and the Zulu

With the king exiled and the army broken, the **Zulu kingdom** was carved up by the British. Sir Garnet Wolseley replaced Chelmsford as the local British commander, dividing Zululand into territories ruled by various pro-British chiefs. This approach undermined any central authority. The result was internal strife and chaos in many areas, as some chiefs fought each other or tried to restore order.

Cetshwayo was eventually allowed to return in 1883, but his power was never the same. Another civil war broke out between rival factions, further weakening the kingdom. By 1887, the British formally annexed most of Zululand. The proud Zulu monarchy lingered in reduced form, with no real independence. These events ended an era in which the Zulu kingdom stood as a major regional power.

6. Wider Effects of the Anglo-Zulu Wars

British Expansionist Goals

The Anglo-Zulu War was part of a broader British drive to control southern Africa. Around the same time, the British had annexed the Transvaal (1877), aiming to rein in both the Boers and local African groups. The destruction of Zulu independence removed a significant obstacle to British plans. It also sent a message to other African polities that defying the empire could lead to harsh consequences.

Some historians argue that the British government in London was less enthusiastic about these costly wars, but local officials like Bartle Frere pushed them forward. Still, once set in motion, the British Empire backed its armies with the necessary supplies, determined not to lose face in front of European rivals. The ultimate success against the Zulu consolidated British claims along the southeastern coast.

African Kingdoms Weakened

The downfall of the Zulu kingdom was a major blow to African political independence in the region. For decades, the Zulu had proved that an African state could stand up to outside forces. Now, with their monarchy dismantled, other communities like the **Pedi** or **Swazi** faced even more pressure to accept treaties or face invasion. The pattern of conquest was not unique—Europeans were doing the same in other parts of Africa during the "Scramble for Africa" in the late 19th century. But in South Africa specifically, the Zulu's defeat marked the end of a powerful independent African kingdom.

Lessons Learned by the Boers

Interestingly, some Boer leaders watched the Anglo-Zulu War carefully. They saw how the Zulu initially surprised and beat a large British column at Isandlwana, revealing that discipline and cunning strategies could overcome better technology if the British were caught in an unprepared state. Although the Boers used rifles and not spears, they took note of the British tactics. This knowledge would play a part in later conflicts between the Boers and the British. For now, though, the Anglo-Zulu War overshadowed many other regional issues, gripping the attention of all who lived nearby.

---

7. Social and Cultural Impact

Stories and Memory

In the aftermath, stories about Isandlwana and Rorke's Drift circulated widely. In Britain, Rorke's Drift became a symbol of heroic defense against overwhelming odds. In Zulu oral history, the triumph at Isandlwana remains a moment of pride, showcasing the kingdom's might. These contrasting narratives highlight how one conflict can be remembered very differently by each side. Monuments and museums later appeared in those battle areas, visited by people interested in this dramatic chapter of history.

For Zulu society, the loss and subsequent partition of Zululand led to the scattering of families, weakening of traditional structures, and more direct colonial rule. Some Zulu families moved to Natal to find work, often ending up as laborers on white-owned farms or in growing towns. This shift was part of the broader story of African dispossession and the movement toward labor migration.

Military Innovations

The Anglo-Zulu War also showcased new military technology, such as rapid-firing Gatling guns, though the majority of British soldiers still used Martini-Henry single-shot rifles. The conflict demonstrated the need for better scouting, fortification, and coordination among columns. Meanwhile, the Zulu effectively used their famous "buffalo horns" tactic for encirclement, though it ultimately faltered against entrenched positions and massive firepower. Military historians have long studied this war for its lessons on tactics, leadership, and cross-cultural combat.

CHAPTER 12

TENSION AND THE ANGLO-BOER WARS

Introduction

Following the defeat of the Zulu kingdom in 1879, Britain strengthened its position in southern Africa. However, it still faced another obstacle to total dominance: the **Boer Republics**, mainly the **Transvaal (South African Republic)** and the **Orange Free State**. The British government and local colonial leaders wanted to bring all territories under a single administrative umbrella (or at least ensure that no independent states would threaten British interests). The discovery of **gold** on the Witwatersrand in 1886 intensified these ambitions. Suddenly, the Transvaal stood at the center of a gold boom, attracting foreign capital and a flood of immigrants—many from Britain.

This chapter delves into the complicated buildup of tensions between Britain and the Boer republics. We will discuss the **First Anglo-Boer War** (1880–1881), which surprised the British with a Boer victory, and then the simmering resentments that led to the **Second Anglo-Boer War** (1899–1902). Though we will not dive fully into modern times, we will explore how these wars shaped politics, society, and the future boundaries of what would later become South Africa.

1. Causes of Friction: The Annexation of the Transvaal (1877)

British Move to Annex the Transvaal

The Transvaal faced economic problems and conflicts with African groups—particularly the **Pedi**—in the mid-1870s. The government under President Thomas Burgers struggled financially and militarily. Seizing the opportunity, Britain's Sir Theophilus Shepstone claimed that the Transvaal was collapsing and required "rescue." In 1877, Shepstone proclaimed **British annexation** of the Transvaal, asserting that it would protect settlers and bring stability.

Many Transvaal Boers resented this move. They saw it as an illegal takeover that ignored their right to self-rule, which had been recognized by the Sand River Convention of 1852. Some Boers cooperated with British officials—preferring stability—but a large faction remained bitter. They believed that once the British had subdued the Zulu, they would turn on the Boers, and indeed, that seemed to be happening.

Boers' Attempts at Redress

In the following two years, Boer leaders such as Paul Kruger and Piet Joubert traveled to London, hoping to convince the British government to reverse the annexation. British officials, however, were not willing to undo Shepstone's action. They believed the Transvaal was best under direct or indirect British control, which would also support their broader strategy of confederation. Frustrated by the lack of progress through diplomacy, some Boers decided to resist forcibly.

2. The First Anglo-Boer War (1880–1881)

Outbreak of Hostilities

By late 1880, tensions reached a boiling point. Boers in the Transvaal formed commando units, raised their old republic flag, and declared independence. British garrisons, spread thin and unprepared, became immediate targets. The conflict that followed is known as the **First Anglo-Boer War** or the **Transvaal War of Independence**.

Boer commandos were small groups of mounted farmers, excellent marksmen who knew the terrain. They often wore plain clothing, blending into the countryside. British troops, by contrast, used more traditional tactics, wearing red or khaki uniforms and marching in columns. This mismatch gave the Boers an edge in guerrilla-style engagements.

Key Engagements and Boer Tactics

Fighting broke out in areas like **Potchefstroom**, **Standerton**, and **Pretoria**. The British tried to relieve besieged forts but found it difficult to maneuver in the open. The Boers laid ambushes, targeting supply lines and small detachments. Their mobility and skill with rifles allowed them to pick off British soldiers from long range. The local population also supported the commandos, providing food and information.

The conflict's most famous battle was **Majuba Hill** (February 27, 1881). A British force under General Colley occupied the top of the hill to threaten the nearby Boer positions. At dawn, a group of Boers climbed the hill's slopes with minimal detection. They surprised the British, who had little cover. Firing with deadly accuracy, the Boers routed the redcoats, and General Colley himself was killed. This **Battle of Majuba Hill** proved the deciding blow, forcing Britain to reconsider its position.

Peace and the Transvaal's Partial Independence

The British government, embarrassed by this defeat and dealing with other global issues, decided to negotiate. The **Pretoria Convention** (1881) and later the **London Convention** (1884) restored the Transvaal's self-government, though under certain British "suzerainty." In practice, the Boers regained control, with Paul Kruger emerging as a key leader. Boers widely celebrated this outcome as a victory for independence, while Britain claimed it still had final say in external affairs.

The war was short, but it left deep feelings on both sides. The Boers had proven they could beat a British force in open conflict if they used their mobility and marksmanship. The British, meanwhile, never forgot the humiliation of Majuba Hill. They accepted the peace agreement for the moment, but the underlying tension remained: the Boers demanded full independence; the British wanted them as part of a larger British-controlled federation.

---

3. The Witwatersrand Gold Boom (1886) and Rising Tensions

Discovery and Impact on the Transvaal

In 1886, prospectors found rich **gold deposits** on the **Witwatersrand**, near what became **Johannesburg**. This changed the Transvaal from a mostly agrarian backwater into a gold-mining hub attracting international attention. Foreign investors, mainly British, poured in money to develop mines. Thousands of **uitlanders** (foreigners), many from Britain, flocked to Johannesburg seeking fortune.

As gold exports soared, the Transvaal government under President Paul Kruger gained wealth from taxes and fees. Public works, railways, and government buildings improved. However, the large population of foreign workers and investors demanded political rights and better city services. Kruger's government, influenced by conservative Boer leaders, restricted uitlanders from voting in Volksraad elections, requiring long residency periods and other conditions.

The Uitlander Issue

This **"uitlander question"** became a focal point of conflict. The Transvaal's leaders feared that granting political power to these mostly English-speaking newcomers would undermine the Boer way of life and invite British annexation. On the other hand, Britain argued that its citizens in the Transvaal were denied basic political representation, fueling calls for intervention.

Cecil Rhodes, Prime Minister of the Cape Colony and a major figure in the diamond and gold industries, saw a chance to bring the Transvaal firmly under British control. He believed that uniting southern Africa under British rule would ensure stability and open new avenues of wealth. In the late 1890s, tensions over these issues grew sharper, with each side unwilling to compromise fully.

---

4. The Jameson Raid (1895–1896)

Cecil Rhodes' Scheme

By 1895, Cecil Rhodes, together with certain allies (including some uitlanders in Johannesburg), plotted a scheme to overthrow the Transvaal government. They hoped local English-speaking residents would rise up if a British force helped them. Rhodes's associate, **Dr. Leander Starr Jameson**, led a small band of about 500 men from Bechuanaland (modern Botswana) into the Transvaal. The plan was to reach Johannesburg quickly, spark an uprising, and topple Kruger.

However, the plot was poorly organized. The promised uitlander uprising did not occur. As Jameson's force marched, Transvaal authorities learned of the intrusion. The Boer commandos easily cut off Jameson's band, forcing them to surrender near Doornkop. This fiasco—called the **Jameson Raid**—was a major embarrassment for Rhodes and deeply angered the Boers, who saw it as proof that the British wanted to grab power by force or trickery.

Fallout of the Raid

The British government in London officially disavowed the Jameson Raid, insisting it was not an authorized action. Yet Boer leaders, especially Kruger, blamed Britain's broader ambitions. Tensions between the Transvaal and Britain soared. Rhodes was forced to resign as Prime Minister of the Cape Colony. The Jameson Raid also stirred patriotic feelings among Afrikaners within the Cape and the Orange Free State, who sympathized with the Transvaal's plight.

Newspapers in Europe reported widely on the incident, framing it as either a bold but foolish escapade or a shameful attempt at imperial aggression. The Kaiser of Germany, in a famous "Kruger Telegram," congratulated President Kruger on thwarting the raid, further irritating British public opinion. The seeds of a larger conflict were now sown.

5. The Drift Crisis and Diplomatic Showdowns

Trade Routes and Customs Disputes

In the late 1890s, there were repeated spats between the Transvaal and British authorities over **railway routes**, **customs duties**, and the control of trade. One notable event was the **Drifts Crisis** of 1895, where the Transvaal government tried to block traffic crossing the Vaal River drifts (fords) unless it used Transvaal rail lines. The Cape Colony believed this violated free trade agreements, raising the threat of British retaliation.

Although some crises were resolved through negotiation, each dispute fueled the perception on both sides that the other acted in bad faith. The Transvaal's Volksraad increased taxes on mining companies, many of which were British-owned, intensifying complaints by influential magnates in Johannesburg.

Attempts at Reform

Under international pressure, Paul Kruger's government made small concessions, such as slightly reducing the waiting period for uitlander franchise (the right to vote). But these changes never satisfied the growing demands from foreigners who wanted immediate political power or from British officials who insisted on full equality for British subjects. Kruger, supported by many rural Boers, believed giving foreigners quick voting rights would effectively hand over the republic to British interests. The two positions seemed incompatible, raising the possibility of war as the only solution.

---

6. The Role of the Orange Free State

Alignment with the Transvaal

The **Orange Free State**, another independent Boer republic, initially tried to remain neutral. However, cultural and familial ties linked its citizens closely with those in the Transvaal. Many Free Staters felt Britain's pressure on the Transvaal threatened their own independence. As tensions escalated, President **M.T. Steyn** of the Orange Free State sided more openly with Paul Kruger.

In 1897, the two Boer republics formed a closer alliance, agreeing that an attack on one would be considered an attack on both. This unity increased the potential scale of any future conflict. Britain, now facing the possibility of fighting both Boer republics at once, began building up troops in southern Africa, even though official statements in London spoke of hoping for a peaceful resolution.

Shared Concerns

Both the Transvaal and the Orange Free State worried that British railways from the Cape or Natal would soon ring them in, making it hard to import supplies or weapons from elsewhere. They also saw how Britain had dealt with the Zulu kingdom, the Basotho, and the Xhosa in the past. The Boers feared a similar fate if they surrendered their independence. Thus, the alliance of the two republics was driven by survival instincts as well as a sense of shared Afrikaner identity.

---

7. Lead-Up to the Second Anglo-Boer War (1899)

The Ultimatum

Throughout 1899, negotiations dragged on. Britain demanded immediate uitlander rights and other reforms in the Transvaal. Kruger offered compromises, but not enough to satisfy the British. Meanwhile, the British continued to send troops to South Africa. By October 1899, the Transvaal government, aware that British forces were gathering in Natal and near the Cape, decided on a bold approach: it issued an **ultimatum**. It demanded the withdrawal of British troops from its borders and threatened war if the British did not comply.

The British refused, seeing the ultimatum as an act of defiance. On October 11, 1899, war erupted—the **Second Anglo-Boer War**, or simply the **Anglo-Boer War**, had begun. The Orange Free State joined the Transvaal in the struggle.

Widespread Fear and Hope

As the war began, Boer commandos moved quickly across borders into British-ruled territories, laying siege to towns like **Mafeking**, **Kimberley**, and **Ladysmith**. Many Boers believed they could secure quick victories like they had in the First Anglo-Boer War. They hoped to force Britain to negotiate, especially if the cost of conflict grew too high. On the British side, officials in London expected a swift triumph, given the Empire's global resources and modern army.

In reality, the Second Anglo-Boer War would last until 1902, becoming a brutal, wide-ranging conflict with devastating impacts on Boer families and African communities alike. We will not delve into its entire modern aftermath, but it is important to note that this second war was far larger, more complex, and more costly than the first. In the period leading up to it, many observers in Europe and America watched with fascination or concern, recognizing that a test of imperial power was about to unfold on the South African veld.

8. Consequences of Tension and Warfare

Economic and Social Effects

Even before the second war began, the tension had reshaped the region. Johannesburg expanded into a major city, overshadowing older Boer towns. The wealth from gold mines created a new class of mine owners and magnates, many of whom had British connections. This transformation caused a social shift in the Transvaal, as Boers were no longer just a community of pastoral farmers. Some remained on farms, while others worked in or around the booming city.

For African communities under Boer rule, the rising tensions meant more restrictions. Pass laws and forced labor practices intensified as the republics sought to keep control. African workers in the mines faced harsh conditions and low pay, fueling resentments that would echo long into the future. Meanwhile, the British-run Cape Colony and Natal also enforced racially biased systems, though each territory had slightly different policies.

Boer Nationalism and Unity

Another major effect was the strengthening of **Boer nationalism**. Leaders like Paul Kruger (Transvaal) and M.T. Steyn (Orange Free State) became symbols of resistance. Afrikaners in the Cape, though they lived under British rule, often sympathized with their fellow Boers across the border. Bonds of language, culture, and religion drew them together. Throughout the 1890s, newspapers, churches, and social groups promoted an Afrikaner identity that transcended state boundaries.

This sense of unity would prove important once the Second Anglo-Boer War began. Although not all Afrikaners joined the fight, many provided moral or material support to the republics. Volunteers traveled from the Cape or from overseas (in small numbers) to fight for the Boer cause. Such unity also led to British suspicion of Cape Afrikaners' loyalty, adding to an atmosphere of distrust that would shape the wartime experience.

---

9. Reflections on the First Phase of the Anglo-Boer Conflict

A Pattern of Confrontation

From the forced annexation of the Transvaal in 1877 to the Jameson Raid of 1895–96, the pattern was clear: the British Empire tried to absorb or control the Boer republics, while the Boers resisted. The short **First Anglo-Boer War** ended in a surprising Boer victory at Majuba Hill, but it only paused the rivalry. The gold boom heightened Britain's interest, and the tension over uitlander rights pushed both sides closer to war.

Limits of Compromise

While there were attempts at negotiation, neither the British nor the Boers found a lasting compromise. British leaders insisted that all British subjects in the Transvaal receive fair treatment. Kruger's government feared that these foreign settlers would overwhelm Boer traditions. Meanwhile, the Orange Free State stood by the Transvaal. As the century neared its end, it became obvious that only a major confrontation would decide who controlled the region's vast resources and political destiny.

CHAPTER 13

THE UNION OF SOUTH AFRICA

Introduction

By the end of Chapter 12, tensions between the British Empire and the Boer republics had exploded into the **Second Anglo-Boer War** (1899–1902). This war was far more destructive than the First Anglo-Boer War. It involved large-scale battles, sieges, guerilla tactics, and scorched-earth policies. When it ended in 1902, both the **South African Republic (Transvaal)** and the **Orange Free State** had lost their independence, becoming British colonies. Yet, within a few short years, Britain took steps that would unite these territories—along with the Cape Colony and Natal—into one political entity called the **Union of South Africa** (1910).

In this chapter, we will explore the Second Anglo-Boer War's key phases and its grim impact on Boer families, African communities, and British forces. We will then examine the peace settlement and how the former Boer republics became Crown colonies. Finally, we will see how Britain and local leaders negotiated the creation of the Union of South Africa, shaping the political future of the region as it moved into the early 20th century.

1. The Second Anglo-Boer War (1899–1902)

Initial Phase: Boer Successes

When war began in October 1899, the **Boers** hoped for quick success similar to what they had achieved in the First Anglo-Boer War. They besieged **Ladysmith** in Natal and **Kimberley** and **Mafeking** on the Cape frontier. Boer commandos, consisting of mounted farmers skilled in marksmanship, advanced into British-held areas with confidence. Early battles in late 1899, known as **"Black Week,"** saw the British suffer serious defeats at **Stormberg**, **Magersfontein**, and **Colenso**. These victories boosted Boer morale and alarmed the British public.

However, Britain quickly responded by sending large numbers of reinforcements to South Africa, including experienced generals like **Lord Roberts** and **Lord Kitchener**. By early 1900, tens of thousands of fresh British troops, armed with modern rifles and artillery, began pushing back the Boer forces. They lifted the sieges of Ladysmith, Kimberley, and Mafeking in early to mid-1900.

British Advance and Boer Shifts in Tactics

With the arrival of Lord Roberts, the British captured **Bloemfontein** (capital of the Orange Free State) in March 1900, then **Johannesburg** and **Pretoria** (major cities of the Transvaal) by June. They declared the Orange Free State to be the **Orange River Colony** and the Transvaal to be the **Transvaal Colony**, both under British administration. Many people in Britain thought the war was practically over.

Yet the Boers refused to surrender. Under leaders such as **Christiaan de Wet**, **Koos de la Rey**, and **Louis Botha**, the Boers switched to **guerrilla warfare**. Small commando units attacked railway lines, supply depots, and isolated British garrisons, then vanished into the countryside. Their intimate knowledge of the terrain gave them an advantage, and local Boer farmers often provided them with food and shelter.

2. Scorched Earth and Concentration Camps

British Countermeasures

Frustrated by the Boers' ability to operate behind their lines, the British adopted a **scorched-earth** policy. They burned farms, destroyed crops, and seized or killed livestock to deny Boer commandos support. Homesteads belonging to Boer families—whether they actively supported the commandos or not—were torched. This strategy aimed to starve the guerillas of supplies and force them to surrender.

Alongside this, the British built networks of **blockhouses** across the countryside—small fortified posts linked by barbed wire—to restrict Boer movements. Thousands of African laborers were conscripted or paid to assist the British in constructing these fortifications.

Civilian Suffering

One of the war's most tragic aspects was the rounding up of Boer women, children, and some African laborers into **concentration camps**. These camps were originally intended as places to hold families whose farms had been destroyed, preventing them from aiding the commandos. But living conditions were poor. Food rations were often insufficient, medical care was limited, and epidemics of measles, typhoid, and dysentery spread quickly. Many died, especially children. Estimates vary, but at least **20,000 to 30,000 Boer civilians** perished in these camps.

African populations also suffered. Many African farmworkers were taken from Boer farms and put into separate camps, where conditions could be equally harsh. Although the exact number of Africans who died in these camps is uncertain, it was significant and often overlooked in early accounts of the war. This cruelty caused outrage in some parts of Britain and the wider world, damaging the moral standing of the British Empire.

3. The End of the War and the Treaty of Vereeniging (1902)

Growing Weariness

By 1901, both sides were exhausted. The Boer commandos, though determined, struggled to find enough supplies. Many families were in camps. British field tactics improved, and the blockhouse system reduced the Boers' ability to move freely. The war's financial cost for Britain soared, and public opinion in the United Kingdom grew uneasy about the conflict's length and the conditions in the camps.

Still, the Boers held out until early 1902. Some of their leaders considered continuing the fight, but the reality was that more families were suffering every day. Also, some Boer generals believed that a negotiated peace might preserve a measure of autonomy for their people in the long term.

Peace Negotiations

Representatives of the Boer republics and the British government began talks at Vereeniging, a small town south of Johannesburg. On May 31, 1902, they signed the **Treaty of Vereeniging**. Key points included:

- The Boers acknowledged **King Edward VII** as sovereign, ending the independence of the Transvaal and the Orange Free State.
- Britain promised to restore self-government to these territories as soon as conditions allowed.
- A sum of **£3 million** was allocated by Britain for reconstruction and to help Boer farmers rebuild.
- Dutch (later Afrikaans) language rights were recognized in schools and courts.
- No immediate voting rights were extended to Africans, a matter left to future local governments.

The war's official end brought relief. Yet the scars of scorched-earth policies, concentration camps, and widespread destruction did not vanish. Boer society had been deeply shaken, and African communities had also experienced displacement and hardship. British troops remained in the new colonies to maintain order and oversee reconstruction.

---

4. Transition to Crown Colonies and Steps Toward Union

The Transvaal and Orange River Colonies

After the treaty, the Transvaal became the **Transvaal Colony**, and the Orange Free State turned into the **Orange River Colony**, both under British control. The colonial authorities began rebuilding railways, farms, and towns. Many Boer leaders, once fierce opponents of British rule, realized they needed to work within the new system to restore stability and protect their communities.

Gradually, Britain moved toward granting these colonies self-government. In 1906, the Transvaal received a constitution allowing a locally elected legislature. **Louis Botha** (a former Boer general) and **Jan Smuts** (another notable Boer leader) led the new government. The Orange River Colony gained similar autonomy in 1907 under leaders like **Abraham Fischer**. This quick restoration of self-rule aimed to heal old wounds and reduce the burden on Britain.

Pressures in the Cape and Natal

Meanwhile, the **Cape Colony** and **Natal**, both older British territories, had their own elected assemblies. The Cape Colony had a non-racial franchise in theory—property-owning men of all races could vote—although, in practice, most African and Coloured people were too poor to meet the requirements. Natal had a smaller white population and had passed laws restricting African rights. Tensions over labor and land persisted in both colonies.

Politicians like **Cecil Rhodes** had once pushed for a grand federation, but that dream faltered after the Jameson Raid scandal. Still, a new generation of leaders, such as **Sir Percy FitzPatrick** and **Lord Selborne**, saw the possibility of uniting the four territories (Cape, Natal, Transvaal, Orange River) into one "white dominion," similar to Canada or Australia within the British Empire. They believed this would ensure political stability and help manage race relations according to their own preferences.

5. Negotiations for the Union of South Africa

The Selborne Memorandum (1907)

A key document that paved the way for union was the **Selborne Memorandum** of 1907, prepared by Lord Selborne (the High Commissioner) and his advisors. It argued that the time was ripe to create a single state, uniting the four colonies under one constitution. According to the memorandum, a union would improve railway management, customs duties, and defense. It would also solve boundary disputes and unify the approach to "native affairs."

White politicians in the Transvaal and Orange River Colony agreed, seeing union as a way to protect their language and culture while sharing power with the Cape and Natal. Leaders from the Cape Colony were generally supportive, though they worried about losing their existing influence. Natal was more cautious, fearing it might become overshadowed by larger colonies.

The National Convention (1908–1909)

From October 1908 to May 1909, representatives of all four colonies met in Durban, Cape Town, and Bloemfontein to draft a constitution. This gathering was called the **National Convention**. Leading figures included **Louis Botha**, **Jan Smuts**, **John X. Merriman** (Prime Minister of the Cape), and **J.B.M. Hertzog** (another important Boer general turned politician).

Key debates included:

1. **Form of Government**: Should it be a unitary state or a federation? After much discussion, they chose a **unitary** model (like Britain) rather than a federation (like the USA).
2. **Representation**: How would seats be allocated in the new parliament? Ultimately, they decided on a House of Assembly with seats assigned by population among the four provinces. A Senate was also created.

3. **Capital**: They settled on a compromise: **Pretoria** as the administrative capital, **Cape Town** as the legislative capital, and **Bloemfontein** as the judicial capital.
4. **"Native" Franchise**: The Cape's non-racial franchise was retained there, but each province could set its own voting laws, meaning the Orange River Colony, Transvaal, and Natal could continue restricting African and Coloured voting rights.

By May 1909, the draft constitution was complete. It was submitted to the British Parliament, which passed the **South Africa Act** in 1909. King Edward VII signed it into law, and the **Union of South Africa** officially came into existence on May 31, 1910—coinciding with the anniversary of the Treaty of Vereeniging.

6. The Birth of the Union (1910)

Structure of the Union

On May 31, 1910, the **Union of South Africa** was formed, combining:

- **Cape Province** (formerly Cape Colony)
- **Natal Province** (formerly Natal Colony)
- **Transvaal Province** (formerly Transvaal Colony)
- **Orange Free State Province** (formerly Orange River Colony, now renamed the Orange Free State again in name but integrated into the union)

The new union had a **Governor-General** representing the British monarch. An elected **Prime Minister** and **Cabinet** governed the country. Parliament consisted of the **House of Assembly** (lower house) and the **Senate** (upper house). Although the union was part of the British Empire, it enjoyed responsible government—meaning it had significant control over domestic affairs.

First Government and Leadership

Louis Botha became the first Prime Minister of the Union, leading a coalition of mostly ex-Boer leaders and some English-speaking politicians. **Jan Smuts** took on important roles such as Minister of the Interior and later Minister of Defense. These men wanted to bridge the divide between Afrikaner and English communities, though they shared a vision of white supremacy in political power.

Many Cape politicians, like **John X. Merriman**, tried to keep alive the principle of a qualified franchise for Black and Coloured voters in the Cape. But the new union constitution allowed each province to keep or create its own rules. Natal, the Orange Free State, and the Transvaal soon passed laws removing or restricting African voting rights. Over time, the non-racial Cape system was also eroded.

7. Impact on Africans, Coloureds, and Indians

Limited Rights

The creation of the union did not improve rights for the majority of the population. Africans, Coloureds, and Indians were generally excluded from meaningful political participation in three of the four provinces. While the Cape's older laws still allowed a small number of Black and Coloured voters, a series of future laws would chip away at this right. The new parliament reserved power almost entirely for white men.

African leaders and communities—such as those who formed the **South African Native National Congress** (in 1912, later renamed the African National Congress)—protested. They argued that Britain's promises of fairness and equality during the Anglo-Boer War negotiations were not being honored. Instead, the Union placed more power in the hands of white leaders who soon passed land and labor laws that hurt African interests.

Extension of Segregation

Even before the union, segregation policies existed in the colonies, but the new government gradually formalized them. Over the next years, the parliament passed laws restricting land ownership by Africans, controlling their movement, and establishing separate living areas. This pattern later grew into the full **apartheid** system in the mid-20th century, though that is beyond our current historical scope. Nonetheless, the seeds of deep racial segregation were already planted in the union era.

8. Rebuilding after the Wars

Economic Reconstruction

After the Second Anglo-Boer War, farms lay in ruin. The British compensation fund helped some Boer farmers rebuild. Many British and foreign investors saw opportunities in gold mining, transport, and manufacturing. Railways linking ports to the interior expanded. Cities like **Johannesburg**, **Pretoria**, **Bloemfontein**, and **Cape Town** modernized. The diamond and gold industries continued to attract migrant labor from across southern Africa, reinforcing the pattern of labor migration and compound housing.

For Boer families who had lost everything, government loans and land resettlement schemes offered a path forward—on condition of loyalty to the new order. Meanwhile, some African communities forcibly removed from their homelands during the war struggled to re-establish themselves. The white-dominated government paid little attention to African farmers' needs, focusing instead on European-settled areas.

Cultural Shifts

In the post-war environment, **Afrikaner identity** began to crystallize. The use of **Afrikaans** (evolving from Dutch) grew in schools and churches, although English remained important in government and business. Many Boers viewed the union as a compromise but believed they could work within it to protect their language and culture. Festivities like **Dingaan's Day** (later renamed Day of the Vow), commemorating the Battle of Blood River, carried new significance, symbolizing Afrikaner resilience.

9. Significance of the Union and Its Legacy

A New Political Framework

The Union of South Africa represented a major turning point. Four colonies with different histories, languages, and laws came together under a single government. This union resolved many colonial-era disputes—about boundaries, railways, customs duties—and formed a dominion under the British crown, similar to Canada or Australia. Yet it also ensured that white rule remained dominant, setting the stage for future struggles over racial justice.

Leaders like Louis Botha and Jan Smuts tried to unify white South Africans—both English and Afrikaner. They hoped to end old animosities from the Anglo-Boer Wars and work toward economic development. However, their approach ignored or suppressed the political rights of the Black majority. This failure to include all peoples in the union's political life would lead to more conflicts down the road.

Path to National Identity

The union laid the groundwork for a "South African" identity that blended British colonial influences and Afrikaner nationalism. Over time, white South Africans of English descent and Afrikaners came to share certain economic and political interests, though cultural tensions would persist for decades. Africans, Coloureds, and Indians were mostly excluded from power, but they also began forming new organizations and networks to challenge discrimination.

Despite the union's major flaws, it shaped the next chapters in South African history. The early 20th century saw the rise of political parties, labor movements, and social changes that tested the union's cohesion. We will explore those developments in Chapter 14, covering **early 20th-century changes and challenges**—including how Afrikaner nationalism grew, how racial segregation hardened, and how the economy adapted to new global pressures.

CHAPTER 14

EARLY 20TH CENTURY CHANGES AND CHALLENGES

Introduction

After the **Union of South Africa** formed in 1910, the new nation faced many difficulties. It had to balance the interests of English-speaking whites and Afrikaners, manage the economy that relied heavily on mining, and address the needs of the majority Black population—whose rights remained largely unrecognized. Over the next two decades, political parties took shape, labor unrest flared, and segregation policies solidified.

In this chapter, we look at the early 1900s up to the late 1920s or so, examining how the fledgling Union handled social, economic, and political issues. We will see the birth of new political movements—some championing Afrikaner identity, others fighting for African rights. We will also explore how World War I (1914–1918) affected South Africa, changing labor dynamics and forging new alliances. By the end of this chapter, we will understand how the foundations of later conflicts and policies were laid during this formative period, though we will not move deeply into modern times.

1. Political Landscape After Union

Louis Botha and the South African Party

Upon the Union's creation in 1910, **Louis Botha** became Prime Minister, leading a coalition that became the **South African Party**

(SAP). Botha's ally, **Jan Smuts**, served in key roles like Minister of Finance and later Minister of Defense. This government aimed to heal rifts between Afrikaners and English-speaking whites, who had been enemies in the Anglo-Boer War less than a decade before.

At the same time, they maintained a firm policy of white supremacy, believing that political power should remain in white hands. The SAP leadership tried to balance English and Dutch (Afrikaans) language interests. They recognized **Dutch and English** as official languages, though Afrikaans was gradually recognized in place of Dutch over the next decades. Botha and Smuts hoped to project an image of unity to the British Empire and the world.

Opposition Voices

Not all Afrikaners trusted Botha and Smuts, feeling they were too friendly toward British interests. A faction led by **J.B.M. Hertzog** accused the government of favoring English speakers at the expense of Afrikaner culture. Hertzog eventually broke away to form the **National Party** in 1914, championing stronger Afrikaner rights and a policy of "South Africa First," meaning less influence from Britain.

On the other side of the racial divide, Black political leaders saw no progress toward including Africans in government. In 1912, they formed the **South African Native National Congress** (SANNC), later renamed the African National Congress (ANC). Although limited in resources at first, it was an important step in uniting African voices against discriminatory laws.

---

2. Racial Segregation Strengthens

Natives Land Act (1913)

One of the earliest major segregation laws was the **Natives Land Act** of 1913. This act restricted African land ownership to designated "reserves," which made up only a small fraction (about 7%) of South Africa's total land area. Africans living outside these reserves had to become labor tenants or wage laborers on white-owned farms. The law aimed to ensure a stable supply of cheap African labor for mines and agriculture, while reinforcing the idea that white farmers controlled most of the country's arable land.

The Land Act caused immediate hardship. African families who had leased land or lived as sharecroppers were forced off properties they had occupied for generations. This led to overcrowding in reserves, increased poverty, and migration to urban areas in search of work. African leaders protested, but the government ignored their pleas.

Urban Pass Laws

Before the union, pass laws existed in some colonies, but the new government expanded them. African men working in towns or on mines often needed **passes** to prove they had permission to be there. If they were found in an urban area without a valid pass, they could be arrested and forced to return to rural reserves or put into labor. These laws controlled African mobility, ensuring a ready pool of low-wage workers but limiting their freedom. Over time, pass laws became stricter, shaping the daily lives of black South Africans in cities.

3. Labor Movements and Unrest

The Mining Industry and White Labor

Gold and diamond mines continued to be the backbone of the economy. But white miners increasingly demanded better pay and working conditions. Trade unions formed among white workers, who wanted to maintain a color bar that reserved skilled jobs for whites, leaving lower-paid, unskilled labor to Africans.

Notable unrest occurred in 1913 and 1914 when white miners in the **Witwatersrand** region went on strike. The government sent in troops to quell the strikes, leading to violence and casualties. These actions underscored the tension between the government's desire for industrial peace and white workers' insistence on protecting their privileged position.

African Workers' Position

Although African workers outnumbered white workers in the mines, they had fewer rights and were barred from forming official unions. When they protested, authorities often responded harshly. Many African laborers came from rural reserves or neighboring countries (like Mozambique, Bechuanaland, and Basutoland). The compound system kept them isolated, and low wages perpetuated poverty.

Nonetheless, small steps toward African worker organization appeared in the early 1920s. Groups like the **Industrial and Commercial Workers' Union** (ICU) later began to unite African workers across different sectors. But in this earlier period, before the 1920s soared, such movements were weak and faced constant government scrutiny.

---

4. South Africa in World War I (1914–1918)

Divisions Over War Participation

When Britain declared war on Germany in 1914, the Union of South Africa was automatically involved, as it was part of the British Empire. Prime Minister Botha and Jan Smuts supported the war effort, sending troops to invade German South-West Africa (now Namibia). Many English-speaking whites agreed, seeing it as their duty to aid Britain.

However, a faction of Afrikaners strongly opposed fighting on Britain's side. They remembered the bitter Anglo-Boer Wars of only a dozen years earlier. Some took up arms in an event called the **Maritz Rebellion** of 1914, led by former Boer generals like **Christiaan de Wet**. Government forces defeated the rebels, and the ringleaders were punished, although with some leniency. This rebellion showed the lingering divide between those Afrikaners who had come to terms with British rule and those who still resented it.

Effects on the Economy and Society

South Africa's economy benefited in some ways from the war, supplying materials and food to British forces. The conquest of German South-West Africa by South African troops ended quickly (1915), expanding the Union's influence. Jan Smuts rose to international prominence, later joining the Imperial War Cabinet in London.

On the home front, African communities did not see any improvement in rights. Though some Africans served in non-combat roles (like labor units), they received no path to equal citizenship after the war. Racial inequalities persisted. And once the conflict ended in 1918, returning white soldiers demanded jobs, further complicating labor dynamics in the mines and factories.

---

5. Afrikaner Nationalism Rises

The National Party (Founded 1914)

During World War I, **J.B.M. Hertzog** officially launched the **National Party** (NP). Its goal was to champion Afrikaner interests and reduce Britain's cultural influence. The NP spoke about protecting Afrikaans as a language and promoting Afrikaner farmers, who often struggled with debt and poor soil. This appealed to many rural Afrikaners who felt left behind by the more pro-British policies of Botha and Smuts.

The National Party also criticized the government's handling of labor strikes and the extension of privileges to English business elites. As a result, the NP began to gain support in the 1915 and 1920 elections, though it did not immediately assume power. It spread messages of Afrikaner unity, drawing on memories of the Anglo-Boer Wars to create a sense of shared suffering and distinct identity.

Cultural Organizations

In addition to formal politics, Afrikaners formed cultural bodies like the **Afrikaner Broederbond** (established in 1918). Though initially small, the Broederbond worked to advance Afrikaners in business, education, and government positions. Afrikaans newspapers and literature flourished, encouraging pride in the Afrikaans language. By the 1920s, Afrikaans was gaining recognition as a separate language from Dutch, taught in schools and used in church services. These developments laid the groundwork for a more organized Afrikaner nationalist movement in later decades.

6. The Pact Government and Shifts in Power

1922 Rand Revolt

Labor unrest surged again in 1922 on the Witwatersrand gold mines. White workers went on strike, opposing wage cuts and the possible inclusion of some Black workers into semi-skilled roles. Strikers clashed with police and government troops, leading to violent street battles in Johannesburg. The revolt was put down forcefully by Jan Smuts, who was Prime Minister by then (after Botha's death in 1919). The harsh response, including bombings by the South African Air Force, shocked many.

This handling of the Rand Revolt turned white laborers against Smuts, accusing him of siding with mine owners. In the 1924 election, a coalition of the National Party (Hertzog) and the Labour Party (Creswell) defeated Smuts's South African Party. This was called the **Pact Government**, bringing Afrikaner nationalists and white labor interests together.

Policies of the Pact Government

Hertzog, as Prime Minister, promoted Afrikaner culture and passed new laws favoring poor white farmers and workers. The government introduced the concept of a **"civilized labor policy,"** giving preference to white workers in government jobs. This approach further entrenched racial segregation in the workforce, leaving Africans in the lowest-paying roles. Hertzog also pushed for the status of Afrikaans in schools and official documents, diminishing English dominance.

However, the Pact Government did not unify all whites. English-speaking business elites worried about being sidelined, though they adjusted because the gold and diamond industries still thrived. For black South Africans, the Pact era meant harsher pass laws and greater limits on movement, reinforcing the color bar in employment and curbing African labor rights.

7. Growing African Protest and Organization

Formation of the ANC

The **South African Native National Congress** (founded 1912) renamed itself the **African National Congress** (ANC) in 1923. Early ANC leaders included **Pixley ka Isaka Seme**, **Sol Plaatje**, and others who wrote petitions, organized delegations, and held meetings protesting racial discrimination. While the ANC was still small and somewhat elitist in its membership, it represented a crucial step toward coordinated African political action.

The ANC campaigned against the pass laws, the Natives Land Act, and the denial of voting rights. However, it lacked mass support in this period, partly because rural Africans were focused on day-to-day survival, and many urban Africans feared retaliation if they joined protests. Still, the seeds of a broader movement were planted, laying groundwork for future decades of resistance.

Other African Initiatives

Aside from the ANC, smaller groups formed, like the **Industrial and Commercial Workers' Union (ICU)**, starting in 1919 in Cape Town. The ICU spread rapidly among dock workers, farm laborers, and others, calling for better wages and an end to oppressive laws. While it achieved some short-term successes, internal splits and government crackdowns weakened it by the late 1920s.

Mission-educated Africans also led social and educational initiatives. Churches and mission schools taught reading and writing, training a small but growing African intelligentsia. These educated Africans challenged the idea that black people were "uncivilized," advocating for equal treatment. Their efforts collided with the government's segregation policies, which aimed to limit black advancement.

8. Economic and Social Shifts

Agricultural Challenges

South African agriculture in the early 1900s faced droughts, pests, and competition from imported goods. Poor white farmers, many of them Afrikaners, struggled with debt and poverty. They often migrated to towns in search of unskilled jobs. The Pact Government introduced subsidies, agricultural boards, and protectionist policies to assist white farmers, further sidelining black tenant farmers.

Urban Growth and Racial Segregation

Cities like **Johannesburg**, **Cape Town**, **Durban**, and **Pretoria** grew rapidly, fueled by mining and industrial expansion. As more black workers moved to urban centers, authorities passed municipal regulations creating racially divided neighborhoods. Early forms of "locations" or "townships" emerged, forcing black residents to live in designated areas. Housing was overcrowded, lacking basic services, while white suburbs benefited from better infrastructure.

This urban segregation foreshadowed later legislation that formalized racial zones. Fear of crime, disease, and "mixing of the races" was used as justification for controlling black urban settlement. Authorities believed that black workers should be "temporary sojourners" in cities, returning to rural reserves once their labor was no longer needed—an idea that shaped labor migration well into the future.

9. Language, Culture, and Emerging Identities

Afrikaans Gains Official Recognition

Early in the 20th century, **Afrikaans** was still often referred to as "Kitchen Dutch." By the 1920s, scholars, writers, and nationalist leaders insisted that Afrikaans was a distinct language. Newspapers, magazines, and literature in Afrikaans grew in popularity. In 1925, the government recognized Afrikaans as an official language alongside English (replacing Dutch). This moment was celebrated by Afrikaner nationalists as a victory for their cultural revival.

Poets and writers such as **C.J. Langenhoven** and **Eugène Marais** gained fame, shaping a literary movement that took pride in Afrikaner heritage. Churches like the **Dutch Reformed Church** conducted more services in Afrikaans, forging a strong link between religious life and language.

English-Speaking Identity

English-speaking whites, many descending from British settlers or new immigrants, maintained close cultural ties to Britain. They often joined clubs celebrating British traditions, read British newspapers, and saw themselves as part of the empire. Over time, however, some identified more as "South African" than purely British, forging alliances with moderate Afrikaners. Yet, language differences remained a sticking point. Schools in Natal and parts of the Cape taught mainly in English, reflecting the region's colonial legacy.

CHAPTER 15

AFRIKANER IDENTITY AND NATIONALISM

Introduction

By the early decades of the 20th century, South Africa's political and social structures were taking shape under the newly formed **Union of South Africa** (1910). White leaders, both English and Afrikaner, worked together in government, but deep cultural differences remained. On one side, English speakers often felt closer to Britain and its empire. On the other side, Afrikaners (descendants of Dutch, Huguenot, and German settlers) held onto memories of the Anglo-Boer Wars, striving to protect their language and heritage.

During this era, a growing sense of **Afrikaner nationalism** began to stand out. This movement aimed to unify Afrikaners, uplift their economic position, and defend the Afrikaans language. Political parties like the **National Party** (NP) and cultural organizations, including the **Afrikaner Broederbond**, played key roles. In this chapter, we will explore how Afrikaner identity evolved, how leaders promoted their cause, and how these efforts influenced life in the Union. We will also see how these ideas paved the way for deeper divisions along racial lines and set the stage for later conflicts.

1. The Roots of Afrikaner Nationalism

Memories of the Anglo-Boer Wars

For many Afrikaners, the **Second Anglo-Boer War** (1899–1902) was still fresh in mind. The British scorched-earth policy and the concentration camps had caused massive suffering. Although the peace settlement allowed the Boer republics eventually to regain self-government (before joining the Union), the trauma left behind a sense of bitterness. Afrikaners felt they had been humiliated and robbed of their independence.

This collective memory shaped the new generation. Parents told children stories of bravery and sacrifice. In rural areas, families remembered the farmland destroyed by British troops. Over time, these memories grew into a kind of national story, uniting Afrikaners who lived on different farms or in separate towns.

The Language Factor

Another force binding Afrikaners was their language—**Afrikaans**. Until the early 20th century, official documents used Dutch, and English was dominant in business and government. But Dutch and Afrikaans had grown apart. Afrikaans was simpler in grammar, with words borrowed from Malay, Khoisan tongues, and other influences. Many Afrikaners spoke it at home and in church.

By the 1910s and 1920s, certain writers, poets, and teachers believed Afrikaans should stand on its own. They published newspapers, magazines, and books in Afrikaans, showing its beauty and depth. Schools slowly began teaching it as a subject. This language revival went hand in hand with Afrikaner nationalism, because many saw Afrikaans as a symbol of their unique identity—separate from the British Empire's influence.

The Church and Religious Bonds

Afrikaners were mostly members of the **Dutch Reformed Church** (DRC) or related denominations. The church played a major role in social life: families attended services weekly, hosted church gatherings, and found moral guidance in sermons. During the Anglo-Boer Wars, church ministers supported families in concentration camps and on farms.

After the wars, these churches became central places to rebuild community ties. Sermons often spoke of Afrikaners as a chosen people with a special destiny, sometimes referencing biblical stories of struggle and deliverance. This religious framing reinforced the idea that Afrikaners should stand firm in defending their traditions. As nationalism grew, the church sometimes supported or encouraged ideals that set Afrikaners apart from other groups.

---

2. Early Political Expressions of Nationalism

The Formation of the National Party (1914)

During the Union's early years (1910 onward), the **South African Party (SAP)** under Prime Ministers Louis Botha and Jan Smuts tried to unify English and Afrikaner whites. But not all Afrikaners trusted them, suspecting they were too close to British business interests. In 1914, **J.B.M. Hertzog** and his allies split off to form the **National Party (NP)**. They accused Botha and Smuts of neglecting the needs of ordinary Afrikaner farmers and laborers.

The National Party platform included:

- **Protecting the Afrikaans language** in schools, churches, and official use.
- **Encouraging Afrikaner farmers**, especially poorer ones, with government support.
- **Reducing British influence** over South African politics, economics, and culture.

Though the NP did not win immediate power, it slowly gained supporters in rural areas, where the memory of the Boer Wars was strongest. As time passed, the NP also attracted some Afrikaners in towns who felt overshadowed by English-speaking elites.

Hertzog and the "Two Streams" Policy

Hertzog, a leading figure in the NP, believed in what he called the "Two Streams" policy. He argued that English and Afrikaners were separate cultural groups that should develop side by side—but remain distinct. Unlike Botha and Smuts, who sought a certain degree of "fusion," Hertzog insisted that each group should maintain its own schools, language rights, and traditions. This approach aimed to ensure that the Afrikaner culture would not be swallowed up by British dominance.

While this might have eased some Afrikaner fears, it also contributed to deeper divides within the white community. English-speakers sometimes felt alienated, worried that they would lose their privileged position if the NP gained full control. Yet, many rural Afrikaners found Hertzog's ideas comforting, as it validated their feelings of difference and pride.

3. Cultural Organizations and the Afrikaner Broederbond

The Afrikaner Broederbond (1918)

A key group in promoting Afrikaner nationalism was the **Afrikaner Broederbond**, established in 1918. Initially small and secretive, it consisted of educated Afrikaner men—teachers, church ministers, professionals—dedicated to uplifting Afrikaner culture and guiding the community's future. The Broederbond believed Afrikaners faced threats from English cultural dominance and from the large Black majority whose labor sustained the economy.

They encouraged Afrikaans-language schooling, published research on Afrikaner history, and placed their members in influential positions—like school boards, local councils, and even church synods. Although the Broederbond was not a political party, it often worked in tandem with the National Party, sharing a vision of a strong, united Afrikaner people. Over time, it became a central network for Afrikaner leadership, expanding its influence into every corner of society.

Cultural Festivals and History

To boost pride, Afrikaner leaders organized festivals, celebrating historical events like the **Great Trek** (1830s) and the **Battle of Blood River** (1838). Monuments—like the **Voortrekker Monument** in Pretoria (though completed only later)—were planned to honor trekker heroes. These commemorations fed the idea that Afrikaners were a distinct nation with a brave past.

School textbooks also began to frame the Great Trek and the Boer Wars as epic struggles for freedom. By teaching children this version of history, nationalists laid foundations for future generations who would see themselves as heirs to a heroic legacy. Many found inspiration in these stories, strengthening their resolve to protect Afrikaans language and identity.

4. Economic Challenges for Afrikaners

The "Poor White" Problem

One driving force behind Afrikaner nationalism was the **"poor white" problem**—the fact that many rural Afrikaners lived in poverty. After the Anglo-Boer Wars, farmland was ruined, and few families had the capital to restore it. Meanwhile, commercial farming became more sophisticated, requiring irrigation and modern machinery that few poor farmers could afford.

Unable to compete, many Afrikaner families sold their farms or lost them to debt and drifted into towns. There, they often lacked the skills to secure good-paying jobs, because many industries preferred English-speaking workers or more experienced artisans. This led to unemployment, social insecurity, and resentment. Afrikaner leaders feared that poor whites could lose their cultural identity or be overshadowed by wealthier English speakers.

Government Intervention

The Union government, especially under Afrikaner-influenced cabinets, introduced measures to help poorer whites. They set up agricultural boards and cooperatives, gave out loans for farm improvements, and promoted Afrikaans as a language of instruction in rural schools. During and after World War I (1914–1918), certain welfare programs emerged to stabilize white families.

From the mid-1920s onward, the Pact Government (a coalition of the National Party and the Labour Party) used policies like the **"Civilized Labor Policy,"** which reserved certain jobs for white workers. This approach improved some Afrikaners' living standards but deepened racial segregation: it systematically pushed Black laborers into the lowest-paying, least-secure occupations.

5. Political Gains and the Pact Government (1924)

The Rise of Hertzog's National Party

In the 1924 elections, dissatisfaction with Jan Smuts's handling of labor strikes and economic struggles propelled **J.B.M. Hertzog's National Party** to victory in coalition with the Labour Party (led by **Frederic Creswell**). This arrangement, known as the **Pact Government**, gave Afrikaner nationalists more power. They immediately pursued policies that promoted Afrikaans and supported poor white workers and farmers.

Hertzog served as Prime Minister (1924–1939), advocating "South Africa First." He insisted that South Africa should not blindly follow Britain's lead in all matters. For instance, the government changed national symbols, emphasizing local identity. In 1927, English and Dutch were replaced on some official forms by English and Afrikaans. By 1928, an official South African national flag (adopted in 1928) replaced the Union Jack in many public places, although the Union Jack still flew alongside it in certain contexts.

Afrikaans Recognition and Institutions

Under Hertzog, Afrikaans gained even stronger recognition. In **1925**, Afrikaans became officially equal to English (replacing Dutch) in parliament and government. Schools received new curricula with Afrikaans textbooks. Universities offered courses in Afrikaans. Meanwhile, newspapers, radio programs, and cultural events flourished in the language. This wave of assertive language policy helped unify many Afrikaners, who now felt they had a government actively backing their cultural aspirations.

6. Social and Racial Implications

Further Segregation Laws

While Afrikaner nationalism uplifted poor whites, it worsened conditions for Black, Coloured, and Indian communities. Hertzog's government passed additional measures limiting African landownership, stiffening pass laws, and restricting job opportunities in skilled trades. The idea of "separate development" gained ground, meaning that different races should live apart and develop their own institutions—though in practice, this kept the Black majority at a severe disadvantage.

For example, the **Native (Urban Areas) Act** (1923) restricted African migration to cities, reinforcing the idea that African people should stay in rural reserves unless the economy required their labor in towns. Municipal councils built separate "locations" or "townships," formalizing racial boundaries. The notion of "influx control"—limiting how many African workers could enter the city—became a key policy tool.

Economic Disparities

White workers, particularly Afrikaners, got a boost from government railways, post offices, and other state enterprises that favored whites in hiring. Meanwhile, African laborers stayed trapped in low-wage positions, sometimes earning only a fraction of white wages for comparable work. This racial wage gap fed into the broader system of segregation.

A small class of black professionals existed—teachers, clergy, doctors, or lawyers—often educated at mission schools or overseas. However, their numbers were tiny. They faced barriers to career advancement and were not welcomed in white professional circles. Although some joined organizations like the **ANC** to push for change, the government largely ignored their demands.

---

7. Growing Afrikaner Identity Through Media and the Arts

Newspapers, Magazines, and Books

Media outlets in Afrikaans multiplied during the 1920s and 1930s. Newspapers like **Die Burger** in the Cape promoted Afrikaner viewpoints, defending Hertzog's policies and highlighting rural stories. Writers and poets published works that romanticized the Great Trek, depicted Boer War heroes, and celebrated farm life. These literary pieces supported the message that Afrikaners had a rich cultural heritage worth preserving.

Afrikaner historians wrote accounts portraying the Boers as pioneers who tamed the wild interior. Though these writings sometimes ignored or minimized African perspectives, they appealed to a shared sense of mission among Afrikaners. This framing reinforced the idea that the Great Trek was a God-guided journey to freedom and self-determination.

Afrikaans Theater and Music

The growth of Afrikaans also touched theater and music. Playwrights staged dramas about trekkers or daily farm struggles, using the Afrikaans language and idioms. Musicians composed Afrikaans folk songs, which people sang at festivals and family gatherings. Church choirs included Afrikaans hymns. All this activity gave everyday people reasons to feel proud of their language and identity, linking them to a broader community that extended beyond their own towns.

Organizations like the **Federasie van Afrikaanse Kultuurvereniginge** (FAK), founded in 1929, coordinated cultural events across the country. They published songbooks (like the **FAK Sangbundel**) that standardized popular Afrikaans tunes, ensuring that distant communities shared the same cultural repertoire. Such cultural exchange created a strong sense of belonging among Afrikaners, whether they lived in the Cape, the Free State, or the Transvaal.

---

8. Conflicts Within the Afrikaner Community

Differences Between Moderates and Extremists

Not all Afrikaners agreed on the same path. Some were moderate, feeling that cooperation with English speakers was necessary for economic stability and global trade. Prime Minister Hertzog, though strongly nationalist, still had to negotiate with English-dominated businesses. He also occasionally worked with leaders like Jan Smuts to keep the Union functioning.

Others were more extreme, believing in complete separation from British influence. These radicals wanted to break ties with the

British monarchy, remove English from official use, and isolate South Africa from foreign entanglements. A handful even admired authoritarian ideas from Europe, especially in the 1930s, as political tensions grew worldwide.

The Fusion Government

In 1933, due to economic problems from the global Great Depression, Hertzog agreed to form a "fusion" government with Jan Smuts's **South African Party** to address the crisis. The new party, called the **United Party**, combined moderate elements from both the NP and SAP. This angered some hardline Afrikaner nationalists, who felt Hertzog had betrayed them by merging with Smuts, a figure associated with more pro-British policies. In 1934, these hardliners, led by **D.F. Malan**, broke away to form the **Purified National Party**—a smaller but fiercely nationalist group.

This split showed that Afrikaner nationalism was not monolithic. Some leaders preferred practical alliances, while others demanded pure ideological positions. Over time, the Purified National Party's unwavering stance on Afrikaner identity would gain traction, eventually leading to a major political shift after World War II.

9. Impact on Broader Society

Continuing Racial Barriers

While Afrikaner nationalism largely centered on white unity, it also contributed to deepening the color line in South Africa. Nationalist leaders believed that uplifting poor whites required reserving skilled jobs and public resources for them. In practice, this meant more laws controlling black people's movements, wages, and residence. Urban locations became more segregated, and pass laws more restrictive.

African resistance movements (like the **ANC**) criticized the new wave of Afrikaner policies, but the government was deaf to these protests. Police often broke up gatherings, and newspapers that supported African rights faced censorship or intimidation. Many black leaders grew frustrated, seeing no avenue for fair political participation. This laid the groundwork for later decades of more intense conflict.

Economic Restructuring and the Depression

The 1920s saw some economic growth, especially in mining and agriculture, but the **Great Depression** (starting in 1929) hit South Africa hard. Exports of gold, wool, and agricultural produce dropped in value. White unemployment rose, and the government scrambled to protect local industries. More regulations and protective tariffs were introduced to shield South African farms and factories from foreign competition. These policies favored white-run businesses, leaving black entrepreneurs with few opportunities and little credit.

Hertzog's focus on Afrikaner welfare meant that the economic pain among poor whites somewhat decreased thanks to government programs, but black unemployment soared without similar assistance. As the Depression wore on, it widened economic and racial divides, while reinforcing the nationalist conviction that Afrikaners needed to stand firm together.

CHAPTER 16

HARDSHIP, ECONOMY, AND THE INTERWAR YEARS

Introduction

Between the end of World War I (1918) and the start of World War II (1939), South Africa faced a mix of economic ups and downs, social stresses, and shifting political alliances. This era is known as the **interwar years.** The country was still a dominion of the British Empire but was governed by its own elected leaders. Industries such as mining (especially gold) and agriculture remained key to the economy, yet global events—like the **Great Depression**—sent shock waves through society.

In this chapter, we look at how economic challenges shaped the lives of ordinary people, both white and black, during the 1920s and 1930s. We will explore the continued push for racial segregation in labor and housing, the role of the government in assisting white farmers and workers, and the rising tensions that eventually led South Africa into another global conflict. We will also see how political alliances formed, broke down, and reformed, influencing the direction of national policy on labor, race, and identity.

1. Post-World War I Adjustments (1918–1924)

Economic Growth and New Problems

After World War I ended in 1918, the demand for South African goods like wool, grains, and minerals initially stayed high. Many European nations needed to rebuild, buying raw materials from abroad. This surge brought profits to some South African farmers and mine owners. In particular, gold mining on the Witwatersrand kept expanding, as gold remained a stable asset internationally.

However, the war had also cut off certain import sources, forcing local businesses to grow their own manufacturing—making textiles, processed foods, and other products. This modest industrial expansion created factory jobs, drawing more people into cities. At the same time, returning white soldiers looked for employment, causing labor competition and pressure on wages.

Social Discontent and White Labor Strikes

The early 1920s saw significant labor unrest among white workers, especially on the mines. White miners feared that employers would replace them with cheaper African labor to cut costs. In **1922**, tensions exploded into the **Rand Revolt** on the Witwatersrand mines. Striking white miners demanded job protection and wage increases, chanting slogans like "Workers of the world unite and fight for a white South Africa!" This showed the strange mix of socialist rhetoric and racist ideas among some white labor groups.

Prime Minister Jan Smuts's government reacted forcefully, using troops and even aerial bombing to suppress the revolt. Many white miners felt betrayed, seeing Smuts as siding with big mining companies. This dissatisfaction helped the National Party (NP) and the Labour Party gain support in the 1924 election, forming the **Pact Government** under J.B.M. Hertzog.

---

2. The Great Depression (1929–1933)

Global Crisis Hits South Africa

Starting in 1929, a severe economic crisis—known as the **Great Depression**—swept the world. Stock markets crashed, banks failed, and international trade collapsed. Although gold exports provided some cushion, South Africa still felt the shock. Demand for other exports—like wool, maize, and fruit—plunged, causing prices to drop drastically.

Farmers faced heavy debt, unable to sell produce at profitable prices. Many white families, already struggling, sank deeper into poverty. The government tried to help by imposing tariffs on foreign goods, hoping to protect local businesses. They also introduced the **Marketing Acts**, allowing boards to control prices of farm products. But such policies mostly benefited white commercial farmers, while smaller or African-owned farms rarely received aid.

Rise in Unemployment and Poverty

Urban unemployment soared as factories cut production. White workers, accustomed to protected jobs, grew angry, demanding the government keep Africans out of certain positions to reduce competition. Meanwhile, black workers, who had even fewer legal protections, lost jobs without any safety net. Some left towns and returned to rural reserves, where land was scarce and overpopulated. Others drifted from place to place, seeking any form of wage labor.

The poverty of black communities worsened under these pressures. Authorities continued to enforce pass laws to control the movement of Africans, often arresting those who traveled to cities without permission. The result was widespread social stress, fueling resentment and activism among the black population, even though their organizations, like the **ANC**, struggled to make big gains in the face of government crackdown.

3. Political Realignments: The Fusion and the Purified National Party

Hertzog and Smuts Unite

As economic woes deepened, Hertzog's **National Party** faced growing challenges. Some felt his government was not doing enough to help poor whites. Yet, moderate Afrikaners and English-speaking conservatives believed that a stable coalition was needed to address the crisis. In 1933, Hertzog surprised many by joining forces with his old rival, **Jan Smuts**, leader of the South African Party. Together, they formed a "fusion" government, eventually creating the **United Party (UP)** in 1934.

This fusion aimed to tackle the Great Depression with coordinated efforts—supporting farmers, stabilizing the currency, and protecting local industries. Hertzog remained Prime Minister, while Smuts took key roles in the cabinet. Their united front reassured big business and foreign investors that South Africa was politically stable. Over the next few years, the economy showed some signs of recovery, partly due to improved gold prices.

Breakaway by D.F. Malan

Not all Afrikaners approved of the fusion. **D.F. Malan**, a minister and newspaper editor, felt Hertzog had betrayed the true spirit of Afrikaner nationalism by merging with Smuts, who was more pro-British. In 1934, Malan led a group of hardline NP members to form the **Purified National Party**. They insisted on pure Afrikaner leadership, total separation from British influence, and a stronger stance on racial segregation.

Though initially smaller, the Purified National Party drew support from rural Afrikaners who distrusted the new United Party. They accused Hertzog and Smuts of forgetting the poor white cause and letting English elites control the economy. Malan's faction would soon become the main voice of uncompromising Afrikaner nationalism, setting itself apart from the "moderate" United Party government.

---

4. Racial Policies During the Interwar Years

Reinforcing Segregation

Even as white politicians argued over fusion or purity, they generally agreed on expanding segregation. The **Native Trust and Land Act (1936)** updated the 1913 Natives Land Act, slightly increasing the amount of land designated for African occupation but still limiting it to about 13% of South Africa's territory. This small expansion did little to relieve overcrowded reserves, and many African families remained landless.

The same 1936 legislation also removed black voters in the Cape from the common voters' roll, placing them on a separate roll with limited representation. This move reversed the Cape's older tradition of a non-racial franchise (though restricted by property requirements). Now, even that small group of property-owning Africans lost direct political power, marking another step toward total disenfranchisement.

Urban Control

Cities introduced more restrictions on African housing, mandating special permits for black families to live permanently in urban locations. Employers often had to sponsor these permits, turning African residents into "temporary sojourners" who could be expelled if they lost their jobs. Government officials argued that controlling African urbanization was necessary to prevent "social problems," but in practice, it kept a cheap, flexible labor force close at hand while denying Africans stable rights to city life.

Among Coloured and Indian communities, discrimination also grew. Laws prevented them from living in certain areas, attending white schools, or sharing public facilities. Though the full system of apartheid was yet to come, the interwar years laid the structural and legal foundations for deeper separation.

---

5. Economic Developments and Industrialization

Mining and Gold Standard

Gold mining remained central to South Africa's economy. During the Great Depression, many countries abandoned the **gold standard**, but South Africa benefited from stable or rising gold prices, as investors sought security in gold. This helped the Rand mines stay profitable, provided tax revenue to the government, and softened some of the worst impacts of the Depression. However, dependence on gold also made the country vulnerable to fluctuations in global markets.

As the 1930s progressed, more capital went into mechanizing mines, improving productivity. White miners tended to hold skilled positions operating and maintaining machinery, while black workers performed underground drilling, carrying, and blasting. The wage gap remained stark: white miners earned multiple times the wages of black laborers, reflecting entrenched racial hierarchies in the workforce.

Growth of Secondary Industries

The government promoted **secondary industries**—manufacturing, food processing, textiles—partly through tariffs and incentives to reduce reliance on imports. Some new factories opened in urban centers, employing both white and black labor. White workers often held supervisory or technical roles, while black workers did basic tasks at lower wages. This shift gradually reshaped society, bringing more Africans into industrial settings and fueling the expansion of urban townships.

For Afrikaner nationalists, building strong local industries was part of the dream of self-reliance and independence from Britain. Some Afrikaner entrepreneurs founded companies producing Afrikaner-themed products or serving Afrikaans-speaking customers. Yet, English-run firms largely dominated big business, including banking, shipping, and large-scale retail. This imbalance further fueled nationalist arguments for more Afrikaner economic empowerment.

6. Urbanization and Housing

Township Expansion

As more people moved to cities for industrial work, local councils forced black families into segregated townships or locations on the outskirts. Areas like **Sophiatown** in Johannesburg or **New Brighton** in Port Elizabeth grew in this period. Housing was often minimal—small, cramped homes without proper sanitation or electricity. Because of pass laws, only officially employed men could legally remain in urban areas, so families were frequently separated.

Despite the hardships, cultural life thrived in some townships. Jazz clubs, shebeens (informal bars), and social organizations appeared. A small black middle class—teachers, nurses, clerks—tried to improve conditions, but faced constant restrictions. Meanwhile, crime and social problems increased in crowded neighborhoods with limited police services or public investment. City officials rarely prioritized black needs.

White Suburbs and Public Services

By contrast, white suburbs grew with better roads, water systems, and public transport. Government funds favored these areas, reflecting the political power of white voters. Middle-class white families enjoyed new forms of leisure—like cinemas, sports clubs, and shopping districts. This stark contrast between white comfort and black poverty became more evident, laying the groundwork for future protest movements.

---

7. The Cultural Scene: Radio, Films, and Literature

Afrikaans Radio

In 1936, the **South African Broadcasting Corporation (SABC)** began radio services in both English and Afrikaans. Radio played a big role in uniting Afrikaner families spread across vast rural areas. Afrikaner nationalists quickly saw its potential to share news, music, and nationalist messages. Listeners could tune in to Afrikaans programs about farming tips, religious talks, and historical dramatizations. This helped strengthen the sense of a shared Afrikaner community.

English-language radio also expanded, featuring British music, news from London, and entertainment programs. In towns and cities, many white listeners enjoyed these broadcasts as a link to the broader empire. Black South Africans had no dedicated radio service at this time; they could only access content in English or Afrikaans, often with no coverage of African affairs from an African perspective.

Films and Books

During the 1930s, imported Hollywood films were very popular among urban whites, showing glamorous lifestyles at odds with day-to-day South African life. A small local film industry tried to produce Afrikaans-language movies, though budgets were tiny. Book publishers released Afrikaans novels that romanticized farm life and retold Boer War tales, again reinforcing nationalist themes.

For black readers, the choices were limited. Some mission-educated Africans wrote newspaper columns or published pamphlets, but few commercial publishers would handle their work. Nevertheless, a handful of black authors emerged, discussing life in the townships, the injustice of segregation, and personal experiences in a rapidly changing society.

8. Political Tensions Leading Toward WWII

Shifts in the United Party

The **fusion** that created the United Party brought a temporary calm to parliament, but ideological rifts continued. Hertzog, though still Prime Minister, grew uneasy about Britain's increasing tensions with Nazi Germany in the late 1930s. He believed South Africa should avoid any future European war, prioritizing its own interests. Smuts, however, felt a moral obligation to stand by Britain if war broke out. These opposing views over foreign policy would soon strain the United Party's unity.

Emergence of Radical Afrikaner Groups

Outside mainstream politics, a few radical Afrikaner organizations, like the **Ossewabrandwag (Oxwagon Sentinel)**, emerged. Founded in 1939, it glorified the Great Trek's centenary celebrations and opposed any involvement with Britain. Some members admired Germany's nationalism under Hitler, seeing parallels with Afrikaner struggles against British imperialism. Although the Ossewabrandwag did not represent all Afrikaners, it showed how discontent simmered among those who felt even Hertzog's policies were too mild.

As World War II drew closer, these radical voices clashed with more moderate figures who saw alliances with Britain as crucial for the country's defense and economic ties. When war finally came in 1939, the question of whether to join Britain would split the government and reshape South African politics once again.

---

9. Social Divides and the Road Ahead

Growth of African Political Awareness

While Afrikaner nationalism dominated headlines, African political groups grew slowly. The **ANC** held conferences, wrote petitions, and tried to cooperate with liberal whites for reform. Yet the government's repressive measures and the general lack of white sympathy hindered progress. A few urban black intellectuals and activists formed grassroots groups to protest poor housing, police brutality, and pass arrests. Although small in scale, these efforts signaled a rising awareness of civil rights.

In the late 1930s, younger African leaders, such as **Anton Lembede** (who would later inspire figures like Nelson Mandela in the 1940s), began to speak of African nationalism. They argued that black people had to rely on themselves to fight oppression, rather than trusting paternalistic gestures from the government. The seeds of a more assertive African nationalism were thus planted during this interwar period, even if they had not yet blossomed.

Indian and Coloured Communities

Indian South Africans, many of whom were descendants of indentured laborers brought to Natal for sugar plantations, faced discrimination in housing and trade licenses. Leaders like **M.K. Gandhi** (earlier in the 1900s) and others tried to negotiate or protest discriminatory laws. Coloured people—of mixed heritage—were also restricted in their political and economic opportunities, often losing the limited voting rights they once had in the Cape. Despite these hardships, local communities tried to build schools, social clubs, and welfare organizations to support each other.

10. Conclusion of Chapter 16

The interwar years were a complex time in South Africa, marked by **economic struggles**, **political splits**, and **social stress**. The Great Depression disrupted livelihoods, forcing the government to enact protective policies for white workers and farmers. While Afrikaner nationalism surged, leading to the formation of breakaway parties like the Purified National Party, moderate leaders briefly worked together in the United Party to manage the crisis.

All the while, racial segregation deepened. Africans saw their land rights curtailed, their voting rights eroded, and their access to urban spaces restricted by pass laws. White solidarity, especially among Afrikaners, came at the expense of black labor, locked into low-wage positions. Industrial growth in the mines and factories accelerated urbanization, yet official planning ensured that black townships remained separate and under-resourced.

By the late 1930s, the rise of **extreme nationalist** Afrikaner groups foreshadowed a new wave of political conflict. At the same time, global tensions built up toward another major conflict—**World War II**. In the next chapters, we will see how South Africa's involvement in that war further shaped domestic politics, boosted industrial expansion, and intensified debates over race and identity. This period sowed many seeds of the future, as the country inched closer to the policies that would define mid-century struggles, though we will continue to stop before fully entering the modern era.

CHAPTER 17

SOUTH AFRICA DURING WORLD WAR II

Introduction

In September 1939, Great Britain declared war on Germany after Hitler's invasion of Poland. As a member of the British Commonwealth, South Africa faced the decision of whether to join the conflict. This choice sparked controversy at home. Prime Minister **J.B.M. Hertzog** wanted to remain neutral, believing the country had its own concerns and should not be dragged into another European war. By contrast, his longtime political partner and rival, **Jan Smuts**, felt a moral and historical obligation to side with Britain. These opposing views split the government, resulting in Hertzog's resignation and Smuts's return as Prime Minister.

Over the next six years (1939–1945), World War II brought big changes to South Africa's economy, society, and politics. Thousands of South Africans served in the military, fighting in East Africa, North Africa, Madagascar, and Italy. The war boosted industry, accelerating manufacturing and urban growth. It also exposed contradictions in the country's racial policies: Black and Coloured soldiers found themselves fighting for freedoms they did not fully enjoy at home. By 1945, the end of the war would leave South Africa poised for new conflicts and debates about race, identity, and sovereignty.

In this chapter, we will look at how South Africa's involvement in World War II affected every part of society. We will examine the political drama surrounding Smuts's wartime leadership, the economic surge driven by wartime demand, and the shifting roles of different communities (white, Black, Coloured, and Indian). Finally, we will see how these wartime developments set the stage for post-war tensions that would soon reshape the entire country.

1. The Decision to Enter the War

Hertzog vs. Smuts and Government Crisis

When Britain declared war on Germany, South Africa had a choice: join Britain or remain neutral. Prime Minister Hertzog argued that the Union should stay out of European quarrels. He proposed a policy of neutrality, claiming it was best for the country's internal stability. However, **Jan Smuts**, Hertzog's partner in the "fusion" government (the United Party), strongly believed in supporting Britain—partly because of ties to the empire, partly due to fear of Nazi aggression.

This disagreement led to a crisis. Hertzog asked parliament to support neutrality. A vote was taken, and members sided with Smuts. Seeing he no longer had the majority, Hertzog resigned in early September 1939. The Governor-General then invited Smuts to form a new government. Smuts became Prime Minister for the second time (his first tenure had ended in 1924). South Africa officially declared war on Germany on September 6, 1939, aligning with Britain's cause.

Public Reactions

English-speaking South Africans generally supported the war effort, sharing cultural and historical bonds with Britain. Many enlisted in the armed forces, proud to fight under the Union Jack. However, significant parts of the Afrikaner population opposed entering another British war, remembering the traumas of the Anglo-Boer conflicts only a few decades earlier. Some formed or joined groups like the **Ossewabrandwag** (OB), which actively criticized the government's pro-British stance.

Black South Africans had varied responses. Some hoped that supporting the war might bring better treatment and more political recognition. Others felt skepticism—why fight for "democracy" overseas when rights at home were restricted? Despite these doubts, many Black and Coloured South Africans volunteered, seeking wages, skills training, or simply an escape from poverty in the reserves and townships.

---

2. Military Involvement and Campaigns

East Africa and North Africa

South Africa's armed forces, modernized under Smuts's direction, deployed first to **East Africa** in early 1940 to fight Italian forces that had occupied Abyssinia (Ethiopia) and Somaliland. South African soldiers served alongside British, African colonial, and other Allied troops. They experienced harsh conditions—heat, disease, rugged terrain—but contributed to Allied successes in pushing the Italians out.

Later, many South African units joined the famous campaigns in **North Africa**, battling German and Italian forces under General Erwin Rommel. South Africans fought in major engagements such as the Siege of Tobruk and the Battles of El Alamein (1941–1942). Though they suffered heavy casualties and faced supply shortages, they played a notable role in eventually halting the Axis advance.

Madagascar and Italy

In 1942, Smuts also sent forces to **Madagascar** to secure it from possible Japanese or Vichy French control. The island's strategic position along shipping routes made it critical to Allied plans. South African troops participated in amphibious landings, capturing key ports. Later, in 1943–1945, some units moved to the **Italian front**, fighting in mountainous regions alongside British and other

Commonwealth divisions. This final phase of South Africa's war involvement was smaller in scale but still demanding, as soldiers contended with winter conditions far from home.

Soldiers of All Backgrounds

Though frontline combat roles were reserved primarily for white troops, Black, Coloured, and Indian South Africans served in support units—transport corps, labor battalions, medical assistants, drivers, and cooks. Some served under the "Native Military Corps," wearing special insignia. They rarely received weapons training, reflecting the racial attitudes of the time. Nonetheless, their work was essential for logistics and supply. Thousands traveled abroad, experiencing different cultures and occasionally glimpsing less-segregated societies, which shaped their expectations upon returning.

3. Wartime Economy and Industrial Boom

Increased Manufacturing

South Africa's economy grew rapidly during World War II, thanks to the high demand for minerals, food, and manufactured goods for the Allied war effort. The Union government set up new factories to produce uniforms, boots, ammunition, and other military equipment. Existing industries expanded, and many new workers—white and black—moved to urban centers seeking employment.

The government established bodies like the **War Supplies Board** to coordinate production and allocate materials efficiently. The shortage of imports from overseas encouraged local entrepreneurs to invest in making items previously imported, such as textiles, chemicals, and machinery. This shift laid the foundation for a more diverse industrial base after the war.

White Labor Protection and Black Workers

While white unemployment dropped sharply due to war production, black workers filled many lower-paid positions in factories and transport. Wartime labor shortages sometimes forced employers to relax color bars, allowing black employees to perform semi-skilled tasks. However, official policies still tried to maintain racial wage gaps and job segregation. The government regulated wages and working conditions, but enforcement favored white employees' interests.

Some black workers joined informal unions or staged small strikes for better pay, often facing harsh crackdowns. Nonetheless, exposure to industrial work gave them new skills and a sense of collective power. Many Africans who had left rural reserves for city jobs became more determined to seek fair labor practices and to question the state's segregation laws—though any push for reform remained limited during the war.

---

4. Social Changes on the Home Front

Urbanization and Housing Pressures

With the industrial boom, cities like Johannesburg, Cape Town, Durban, and Pretoria swelled. White workers often found improved housing due to government or employer schemes. But black migrants had no such support. They crowded into existing townships, leading to severe housing shortages. Municipalities responded by setting up basic hostels or barracks for single male workers. Families struggled to find proper accommodation, creating a spike in informal shanty areas.

Pass laws tightened further to control this influx, and police raids became frequent. Despite these hardships, many black families found war-related jobs better than rural poverty. The result was a more permanent black urban presence, even though official policy still treated black workers as "temporary sojourners" expected to return to rural reserves once no longer needed by industry.

Role of Women

White women increasingly worked in offices, banks, and factories, replacing men who had gone to war. Some joined women's auxiliary services in the military, serving as clerks, typists, drivers, or nurses. These roles expanded women's horizons. Yet, once the war ended, many were expected to give up jobs so returning male soldiers could be rehired.

For black and Coloured women, the options were fewer. Domestic service continued to be a common occupation, though a minority found factory work. Migrant labor restrictions and patriarchal traditions meant many black women remained in rural areas, caring for children while husbands went to towns or to the military. Those in urban townships often did informal sector jobs (laundry, beer-brewing, street vending) to survive.

---

5. Political Tensions and the Ossewabrandwag

Anti-War Sentiments

Throughout the war, a portion of Afrikaners remained openly hostile to the Smuts government's alliance with Britain. The **Ossewabrandwag (OB)** was formed in 1939 as a cultural organization commemorating the Great Trek's 100-year anniversary. But it soon evolved into a movement with strong anti-British and, in some cases, pro-German sympathies. Members disliked the idea of fighting on the side of the empire that had once brutalized the Boer republics.

The OB organized rallies, paramilitary drills, and sometimes sabotaged war-related infrastructure. The government cracked down, arresting leaders and interning hundreds of activists. This conflict highlighted how the war reignited old Anglo-Boer hostilities. Prime Minister Smuts himself had to dedicate resources to domestic security, though the majority of Afrikaners either supported the war or stayed neutral rather than joining militant groups.

Smuts's Balancing Act

Jan Smuts worked hard to maintain unity. He realized that pushing Afrikaner dissenters too harshly could fan the flames of rebellion. So, while clamping down on direct sabotage, he also used softer approaches, letting some critics speak freely if they did not advocate violence. This careful balancing helped Smuts keep overall control and ensure South Africa continued its contribution to the Allied war effort.

Meanwhile, other political factions maneuvered for post-war influence. D.F. Malan's **Purified National Party** avoided open sabotage but campaigned against the war, presenting itself as the true defender of Afrikaner interests. As casualties rose and sacrifices mounted, more Afrikaner voters leaned away from Smuts's pro-British stance.

6. Impact on Racial Politics and African Hopes

Black Soldiers and Civil Rights

Though most black soldiers served in non-combat roles, many returned from war expecting greater recognition at home. They had endured the same dangers as white troops, assisted in Allied victories, and seen countries where racial barriers were less rigid. Some believed that if the war was about defending freedom against tyranny, it should also mean advancing rights for black South Africans.

However, the government's official line was that black soldiers should not expect new political privileges. Upon demobilization, they found the same pass laws and color bars. Disappointment ran deep. This experience laid the foundation for future activism. Younger black veterans often joined or strengthened organizations like the **ANC**, determined to challenge segregation more vigorously.

Coloured and Indian Communities

Coloured and Indian South Africans, many of whom had also contributed to the war effort in support or labor roles, gained little from victory. They remained subject to discriminatory laws on residence and employment. Some Indian activists referenced India's independence movement, hoping that Britain's promises of "freedom" and "self-determination" would mean reforms in South Africa too. But the Smuts government offered only token changes, such as minor improvements in local representation, which fell far short of real equality.

---

7. Economic and Social Outcomes at War's End

Post-War Prosperity and Inequality

World War II boosted South African manufacturing, mining profits, and job creation. At the war's end in 1945, the country's industries were stronger and more diverse than before. The gold sector remained a cornerstone, bringing in foreign currency. White living standards, on average, rose with new skills and higher wages. More white families moved into suburban homes, bought cars, and enjoyed consumer goods.

Meanwhile, black urban populations expanded, with tens of thousands locked in poorly funded townships. They faced limited health care, education, or public utilities. The wage gap between black and white workers, already large, often widened. Racial policies had hardened, ensuring that white South Africans reaped the bulk of post-war economic gains, while black, Coloured, and Indian communities remained in poverty or near-poverty conditions.

The Rise of Smuts and Decline of Hertzog

As the war ended, Jan Smuts appeared to stand tall. He was recognized internationally for his contributions to Allied strategy and his role in founding the **United Nations** in 1945. He traveled abroad, meeting global leaders. At home, though, not everyone admired him. Afrikaner nationalists saw him as a collaborator with Britain, ignoring Afrikaner needs. Hertzog's influence had waned, overshadowed by new nationalists like Malan, who pressed a more radical Afrikaner-first approach.

---

8. Political Shifts and the 1948 Election

Prelude to a New Era

In the immediate post-war period, Smuts remained Prime Minister, leading the United Party. He and his cabinet hoped that the country's war record would unify whites behind a moderate approach. They even floated mild reforms for labor or race relations, but nothing significant materialized. The **Purified National Party**, rebranded simply as the National Party (NP), had been growing quietly, forging alliances with other Afrikaner groups. They built a platform of strict racial segregation—what they called **apartheid**—and intense Afrikaner cultural promotion.

Many white voters, especially rural Afrikaners, resented the high cost of war, the presence of black workers in towns, and the overshadowing of their culture by the English-speaking elite. They blamed Smuts for not fully defending Afrikaner interests. They also feared that the mild liberal tendencies in the United Party might lead to demands for black political rights.

The Surprise Victory

In 1948, the next general election took place. Smuts's United Party ran on a platform of gradual improvement and continued moderate race policies. The National Party, led by **D.F. Malan**, hammered home the message of "swart gevaar" (black danger) and the need for a total system of racial separation. They promised to protect jobs for whites, clamp down on black mobility, and restore Afrikaner pride.

To the astonishment of many observers, the NP won a narrow victory in parliamentary seats, though they did not gain a majority of the popular vote. This result ushered in **Malan** as Prime Minister and spelled the end of Smuts's era. The new government wasted no time in solidifying the pillars of apartheid—a system far more extensive than prior segregation. Though we will not delve deeply into modern times, it is important to note that this 1948 election was a direct outcome of wartime transformations and the growing Afrikaner nationalist wave.

CHAPTER 18

POST-WAR SHIFTS AND GROWING DIVISIONS

Introduction

World War II had ended in 1945, and South Africa emerged with an expanded industrial sector, a growing urban population, and a sharp divide in white politics. **Jan Smuts**, hailed worldwide for his contributions to the Allied cause, lost the 1948 election to **D.F. Malan's National Party (NP)**—a stunning shift that heralded a new phase of racial policy. Although segregation had long existed, the NP aimed to formalize and strengthen it under the banner of **"apartheid."**

In this chapter, we will explore the immediate post-war period (roughly 1945 to the early 1950s), focusing on the social, economic, and political realignments that occurred. We will see how African, Coloured, and Indian communities experienced the tightening grip of racially defined laws. We will also examine the efforts of new and existing political groups—like the **ANC**—to challenge these developments, even as the government consolidated power. Finally, we will consider how Afrikaner nationalism and white fear of black urban growth combined to drive a more systematic approach to racial separation.

1. The 1948 Election and Malan's Government

The Surprise Victory Revisited

As described in the last chapter, the **National Party** won the May 1948 election by securing more parliamentary seats than Smuts's

United Party, even though the UP had a higher overall vote count. This outcome was possible because of how electoral districts were drawn, giving rural constituencies—dominated by Afrikaners—greater weight. Many English-speaking whites were shocked, believing Smuts's global stature made him unbeatable. But Afrikaner nationalists were jubilant, declaring that the Afrikaner volk (people) had reclaimed power.

Key Figures: Malan and Strijdom

Reverend **Daniel François Malan** became Prime Minister, leading a cabinet determined to entrench white minority rule. Alongside him stood influential party members like **J.G. Strijdom**, who championed ultra-conservative racial policies, and **Hendrik Verwoerd**, the ideologue behind apartheid's theoretical framework (Verwoerd would rise to greater power in the late 1950s). Malan's administration immediately announced plans to refine and enforce segregation more systematically, calling it "apartheid," meaning "apartness" or "separateness" in Afrikaans.

The Initial Steps

In the first months, Malan's government consolidated control over institutions. They replaced senior civil servants loyal to Smuts, put NP supporters in key police and bureaucratic roles, and initiated commissions to study "race issues." Publicly, they claimed to ensure "separate development" for each race, but critics—both local and international—saw it as a blueprint for intensifying discrimination. Meanwhile, English-speaking industrialists and financiers sought to maintain business continuity, hoping the new government's racial policies wouldn't harm profits.

2. Racial Legislation Takes Shape

Population Registration and Group Areas

Although the full suite of apartheid laws would unfold through the 1950s, the seeds were planted right after 1948. The **Population Registration Act** was drafted, requiring every person to be classified by race: White, Coloured, Bantu (African), or Indian. This classification determined which neighborhoods people could live in, which schools they could attend, and what jobs they might hold.

The government also introduced proposals for **Group Areas** legislation, seeking to assign entire residential areas to one racial group. Mixed neighborhoods, which had existed in older parts of Cape Town, Johannesburg (like Sophiatown), or Durban (like the Indian Quarter), faced forced removals. Although the comprehensive Group Areas Act only became law in 1950, the planning and discussion took root immediately. The idea was to push Black and Coloured residents out of central city zones into segregated townships or distant "homelands."

Banning of Mixed Marriages

Even before 1948, social taboos against interracial relationships existed, but Malan's government wanted them stamped out by law. Draft legislation on **Mixed Marriages** and **Immorality** Acts forbade Whites from marrying or having sexual relations with non-Whites. The justification was to "protect racial purity" and reflect "Christian-national" values. This approach mirrored some extremist ideologies from Europe in the 1930s, though post-war global sentiment was generally against racial discrimination. Still, the NP pressed on, driven by fear of losing white cultural dominance in a majority-black country.

3. The Fate of Smuts's United Party

Disarray and Opposition

After the election defeat, **Jan Smuts** served as opposition leader briefly. His advanced age and disappointment at losing overshadowed his final years in politics. When he died in 1950, the United Party lost its central figure. A new generation tried to reorganize, but they struggled to formulate a strong alternative to apartheid. Many UP members agreed that some form of segregation was necessary; they merely opposed the NP's more extreme measures.

As a result, white parliamentary opposition to Malan's program remained mild. The United Party criticized forced removals or certain harsh laws, but never advocated broad equality for Africans. This lukewarm stance left the NP free to pass discriminatory laws with minimal white political resistance. The English press occasionally protested the new policies, but economic elites mostly adapted, focusing on business interests.

English-Afrikaner Relations

Though Afrikaners now held state power, English speakers continued to dominate finance, large industry, and some media. Both groups were white and thus shared a common interest in preserving political control. Over time, NP leaders reassured big business that a stable racial hierarchy would ensure cheap labor and prevent social upheaval. Many English-speaking industrialists were content to let the NP handle "native policy," as long as commerce thrived. This silent partnership between Afrikaner politicians and English capitalists was key to sustaining the system.

4. Growing African Resistance

ANC Youth League and New Voices

During WWII and in the immediate post-war years, a younger generation of African activists criticized the **African National Congress (ANC)** for being too cautious and elitist. Figures like **Anton Lembede**, **Nelson Mandela**, **Oliver Tambo**, and **Walter Sisulu** formed the **ANC Youth League** in the mid-1940s. They believed in African self-reliance and direct action.

With the NP's rise to power in 1948, these younger leaders found fresh urgency. They argued that mild petitions or polite delegations would not stop the new apartheid onslaught. They called for mass mobilization—strikes, boycotts, protests, and alliances with other oppressed communities. However, they faced the challenge that the older ANC leadership still preferred moderate methods, worried about provoking violent crackdowns.

The Indian and Coloured Response

Indian political organizations like the **South African Indian Congress** (SAIC) also stepped up protests against segregated trading licenses, schooling, and residential restrictions. Leaders such as **Yusuf Dadoo** and **Monty Naicker** advocated cooperation with African groups, forming what became known as the "Doctor's Pact" with the ANC. Coloured communities, under groups like the **Anti-CAD (Coloured Affairs Department)** movement, also resented the new classification laws that threatened their neighborhoods. However, each group struggled with internal divisions and limited resources.

Challenges Facing Resistance

The state's security apparatus was strong, with police cracking down on gatherings, arresting activists, and using pass law violations to keep thousands in line. Additionally, racial barriers hindered a united front among Africans, Coloureds, and Indians. Distrust lingered due to historical divides. Still, the seeds of multi-racial cooperation were evident, foreshadowing future alliances against apartheid. But in this immediate post-war period, these efforts were small sparks rather than a large-scale flame.

---

5. Economic Shifts and Urban Realities

Continued Industrial Growth

Even after WWII ended, South Africa's economy maintained momentum. International markets valued gold, and new manufacturing sectors kept expanding. Infrastructure projects—like roads, railways, and ports—were upgraded to handle increased trade. White unemployment stayed low, and Afrikaner farmers benefited from price controls and subsidies. Meanwhile, the state funneled more resources into developing "Afrikaner businesses," sometimes awarding government contracts to NP-aligned entrepreneurs.

Black workers found jobs in factories, construction, and service industries, but faced wage discrimination and limited advancement. Women of all races participated more in the labor force, though white women had better prospects in office jobs, while black women were channeled into domestic work or labor-intensive factory tasks. Migrant labor from rural reserves or neighboring territories (like Basutoland, Bechuanaland, and Mozambique) remained essential to mines and farms.

Township Expansion and Social Pressures

Cities like Johannesburg, Pretoria, and Cape Town expanded outward, building new white suburbs with paved roads, electricity, and amenities. Black townships (e.g., Soweto outside Johannesburg, Langa outside Cape Town, and others) also grew, but under strict municipal oversight. Housing was often substandard, crowded, and lacked essential services. Government officials believed urban Africans should remain temporary, thus discouraging permanent housing solutions.

Pass raids became more frequent, as police tried to enforce influx control. In response, community leaders set up local committees to protest living conditions, though such efforts rarely moved the authorities. Some black workers formed clandestine unions to demand better wages. A few smaller strikes erupted, but the threat of losing jobs or being deported to rural areas often forced concessions.

6. Afrikaner Nationalism in Action

Cultural Programs

Malan's government poured funds into Afrikaner cultural projects. Afrikaans-language schools received better facilities, universities like Stellenbosch and Potchefstroom expanded programs in Afrikaans, and state broadcasting in Afrikaans increased. Monuments celebrating the Great Trek and the Anglo-Boer Wars multiplied, further feeding a sense of proud Afrikaner heritage.

The **Afrikaner Broederbond**, though not officially part of the government, maintained close ties with NP leaders. Broederbond members filled civil service posts, influenced educational curricula, and shaped public policy to favor Afrikaner interests. They published newspapers and magazines that backed apartheid ideology, claiming it was a moral solution that respected "each group's identity."

Economic Empowerment for Afrikaners

Under the NP, state-owned corporations (like the railway system, electricity provider Eskom, and steel giant ISCOR) were encouraged to hire Afrikaners in management and skilled roles. Government loans and grants helped Afrikaner farmers modernize. The NP's industrial boards promoted Afrikaner-owned businesses, giving them preferential contracts. This active empowerment policy aimed to close the gap between Afrikaans-speaking and English-speaking whites, many of whom had historically controlled commerce and finance.

By the early 1950s, the gap in white incomes was narrowing. More Afrikaners entered white-collar professions, moved into suburban homes, and felt pride in their government's achievements. This reinforced loyalty to the NP, even as the moral implications of apartheid became clearer globally.

7. International Reactions and Challenges

Post-War World Mood

After WWII, the global community embraced ideas of human rights, culminating in the **Universal Declaration of Human Rights (1948)**. Anti-colonial movements swept Asia and Africa, with India gaining independence in 1947 and other territories seeking self-governance. Many countries and activists abroad questioned South Africa's intensifying racial laws, viewing them as out-of-step with the new emphasis on equality and freedom.

While Britain maintained an uneasy alliance due to historical ties and economic interests, some British politicians criticized apartheid behind closed doors. The United Nations (UN), where Jan Smuts had once been celebrated, increasingly hosted debates about racial discrimination. However, the NP government dismissed external criticism, claiming sovereignty over internal affairs.

Neighbors and African Nationalism

In southern Africa, Britain still controlled territories like **Bechuanaland (Botswana), Basutoland (Lesotho),** and **Swaziland (Eswatini).** Portuguese colonies, such as **Mozambique** and **Angola,** remained under rigid colonial rule, while Rhodesia (now Zimbabwe) was under white minority control. This environment meant South Africa did not stand out as the only place with segregation—but its new apartheid policies were more explicit and comprehensive, drawing growing condemnation from certain African and Asian states at the UN.

---

8. Shifts in African, Coloured, and Indian Politics

The ANC's Program of Action (1949)

Under pressure from its Youth League, the ANC in 1949 adopted a bold **Program of Action** advocating mass protests, boycotts, and strikes. Leaders like **Nelson Mandela, Walter Sisulu,** and **Oliver Tambo** urged the organization to leave behind its older cautious approach. They reasoned that only sustained popular resistance could stop the NP's apartheid project.

Even with this program, the ANC struggled to mobilize large numbers. Fear of repression, plus the reality of everyday survival needs, limited immediate results. Still, the groundwork was laid for future campaigns. Alliances with the Indian Congress and some Coloured organizations gained traction, hinting at a united front in the early 1950s.

Indian and Coloured Responses

Coloured communities saw their representation in the Cape Province threatened by new laws that aimed to remove them from the common voters' roll. Protests arose, but the NP insisted that Coloured voters should have separate representation, effectively reducing their impact. Indian leaders protested forced resettlements in Natal, especially around Durban, where Indian-owned properties faced confiscation if they were in "white areas."

Despite these grievances, the government plowed ahead, passing laws that restricted property ownership, banned interracial unions, and tightened pass regulations for Africans. By the early 1950s, these measures formed a patchwork of oppressive rules that future historians would label the bedrock of "petty apartheid" and "grand apartheid."

9. Economic Outlook and Social Tensions

Industrial Advancement, Racial Contradictions

The manufacturing sector continued to expand, creating demand for semi-skilled labor. Even though official policy insisted on strict color bars, some factories quietly trained black workers in roles once reserved for whites, driven by cost savings and labor shortages. This contradiction—economic needs vs. racial ideology—would remain a source of tension, as the NP tried to balance the demands of business with the party's segregation platform.

Urban black populations kept growing, forcing the government into more aggressive measures. Shack settlements mushroomed on city edges, leading to health crises, crime surges, and protest over living conditions. Police raids on "illegal squatters" became a regular occurrence, fueling anger in communities.

White Unity and Division

White South Africans still enjoyed strong job security, rising wages, and social privileges. Even so, subtle divisions lingered between

English speakers and Afrikaners. Some English-speakers disliked the NP's open racial theories, embarrassed by negative press overseas. Others took a pragmatic stance—accepting apartheid to maintain white supremacy, or simply ignoring politics in favor of personal advancement. Afrikaner nationalists, meanwhile, consolidated power in the civil service, schools, and media, building a more cohesive sense of "Afrikanerdom."

By the early 1950s, this relative unity among whites contrasted sharply with the massive, unrepresented black majority. The stage was set for deeper conflicts down the line.

CHAPTER 19

SEGREGATION POLICIES BEFORE APARTHEID

Introduction

Throughout our previous chapters, we have seen how racial divisions in South Africa shaped social, economic, and political life. Long before the official **apartheid** system was introduced by the National Party in 1948, there were already **segregationist policies** that controlled where people could live, which jobs they could have, and how they could participate in society. These policies often grew piece by piece, influenced by labor demands, land grabs, and the desire of white leaders to maintain power over the Black majority.

In this chapter, we will take a closer look at **segregation policies before apartheid**. We will see that many laws—such as early pass regulations, land acts, and urban control measures—laid the groundwork for the harsher rules of the post-1948 era. By studying these earlier policies, we understand how South Africa's racial order did not appear suddenly but was built over decades of smaller steps. By the end of this chapter, you will see how the concept of "separate development" had roots well before the National Party's official introduction of the term "apartheid."

1. The Roots of Segregation in the Late 1800s

Early Pass Laws

From the earliest days of Dutch and British colonization, **pass laws** were used to control the movement of African people. Initially, these passes or "tickets" made sure that Africans employed on farms or in towns could not easily leave or seek other opportunities. In the 19th century, as **diamond** and **gold** mining boomed, mine owners and governments strengthened these pass systems. They wanted a steady supply of cheap labor, making it illegal for Africans to travel without official documents. Failure to carry a pass often resulted in arrest or forced labor.

By the late 1800s, the idea that Africans should live in separate areas from whites—either in rural reserves or in designated urban "locations"—was already forming. Officials in places like the **Cape Colony**, **Natal**, and the **Transvaal** introduced local bylaws separating Black people from white residential zones. These measures were often justified as "sanitation" or "public health" concerns, but they aimed to keep Africans out of white areas unless they worked there.

Tensions Over Land

Land ownership was another early source of segregation. White settlers, especially after the **Great Trek**, occupied vast tracts of land, displacing African communities. By the late 1800s, Boer republics like the **Transvaal** and the **Orange Free State** restricted African land ownership severely. Even under British rule, Africans found it very hard to buy land near towns or in prosperous farming regions. These practices, though not yet formalized by national laws, set patterns that would be codified later.

---

2. Union of South Africa and the First Segregation Measures

Union and Racial Order (1910–1920s)

When the **Union of South Africa** was formed in 1910, uniting the **Cape**, **Natal**, the **Transvaal**, and the **Orange Free State** under one government, the stage was set for more uniform racial policies. White leaders—both English-speaking and Afrikaner—agreed on the need to control the Black majority. They feared that if Africans moved freely to towns and competed for skilled jobs, white wages and living standards might drop.

One of the earliest major segregation policies after Union was the **Mines and Works Act (1911)**, which introduced "color bars" in mining and related industries. It reserved certain skilled jobs for whites, forcing Black workers into lower-paid, less secure positions. This ensured that even as the mining industry grew, most benefits went to white employees.

The Natives' Labour Regulation Act (1911)

Around the same time, laws like the **Natives' Labour Regulation Act** tightened pass requirements. Employers needed to register Black workers, limiting their mobility. If a worker left his job without permission, he could be arrested for violating pass regulations. Such acts reinforced the idea that Black labor could be strictly managed for the benefit of white-run farms, mines, and factories.

3. Landmark Legislation: The Natives Land Act (1913)

The 1913 Land Act

Among the most significant pre-apartheid segregation laws was the **Natives Land Act of 1913**. This act reserved about 7% of South Africa's land for African occupation, even though Africans comprised the majority of the population. Africans were prohibited from buying land outside these "reserves," except in very limited circumstances. Likewise, whites could not sell land to Africans in the "white" areas.

The Land Act immediately disrupted African farming practices. Many African families who had leased or shared land with white landowners were forced off properties they had occupied for generations. Overcrowding in the reserves became severe, leading to soil erosion and declining agricultural yields. People thus often had no choice but to seek migrant labor jobs in towns or mines, which benefited employers seeking cheap labor.

Responses and Protests

African leaders, such as those in the **South African Native National Congress** (later ANC), protested the Land Act. Figures like **Sol Plaatje** wrote about the hardships it caused, explaining how entire communities were uprooted. However, the government dismissed these complaints, insisting that "separate areas" were necessary for peaceful relations. The Land Act thus stood as a cornerstone of segregation, shaping rural life for decades to come and foreshadowing the "homelands" policy under apartheid.

---

4. Urban Segregation and the Natives (Urban Areas) Act (1923)

Growing Towns and Fear of "Swamping"

As mining and manufacturing expanded in the early 20th century, more Africans moved to cities like **Johannesburg**, **Pretoria**, **Durban**, and **Cape Town**. White citizens and officials worried that these rapidly growing African populations would "swamp" white neighborhoods. Health concerns, along with racial prejudice, led municipalities to propose segregated "locations" for Africans, away from central business districts.

The **Natives (Urban Areas) Act of 1923** formalized this approach. It required local authorities to set aside separate living areas for Black residents in or near towns. African men seeking urban work had to live in these areas, usually under the watch of location superintendents. The Act also introduced pass controls for Africans, ensuring they could be evicted if they became unemployed or broke municipal rules.

Impact on Family Life

In practice, these urban townships or "locations" rarely had good facilities. Housing was often overcrowded, lacking adequate water, sanitation, or electricity. The Act assumed that Africans should be temporary sojourners, not permanent city dwellers. As a result, many men lived in single-sex hostels or small rooms, while their families remained in rural reserves. This separation of families had damaging social consequences. Yet, the government cared more about having a stable pool of labor than about African welfare.

5. Labor Control and the Colour Bar

Mines and Works Amendment Acts

Following the initial **Mines and Works Act (1911)**, later amendments (for instance, in 1926) strengthened the **"colour bar"** that kept high-paying skilled roles for whites. White trade unions lobbied fiercely for these protections, fearing that if Black workers gained skills, they would accept lower wages and undercut white labor. These policies, while benefiting white workers, locked Blacks into menial tasks with minimal pay. Over time, this artificially stunted the development of Black skills and professional advancement.

The Wage Gap

The "colour bar" widened the wage gap between white and Black workers. Even as factories and mines expanded, Black employees could not legally perform certain tasks or advance into supervisory roles. White workers, meanwhile, gained job security, decent wages, and union backing. This skewed structure fueled white workers' support for segregation, as it preserved their privileged status. In turn, business owners relied on cheap Black labor for profits, further entrenching the racial division of labor.

---

6. The 1930s: Further Consolidation of Segregation

Native Administration Act (1927)

Though passed in the late 1920s, the **Native Administration Act** grew more influential in the 1930s. It gave the government broad powers over African affairs, including the authority to remove entire communities if officials deemed it necessary for "public interest." It also set up a separate legal system for Africans, with the **Native Commissioner's Courts** applying "customary law" in some cases. Essentially, the Act treated Africans as subjects under a different set of regulations, limiting their access to normal courts.

For white leaders, this legislation simplified controlling a large Black population by placing them under distinct administrative rules. For Africans, it meant less legal protection and a sense that they were governed by a parallel, subordinate system. Over time, these administrative controls built a bureaucratic framework that the apartheid regime would later expand.

Hertzog's "Civilized Labour Policy"

In the 1920s and 1930s, Prime Minister **J.B.M. Hertzog** introduced policies favoring "civilized labour," meaning jobs reserved for whites on state railways, public works, and government services. Afrikaner workers, in particular, benefited from these measures, which aimed to address the "poor white" problem. While it helped many impoverished Afrikaners find steady employment, it also further excluded Black jobseekers, reinforcing the idea that certain sectors should remain white-only.

By the late 1930s, South Africa was well on its way to formal racial division, even though the word "apartheid" had not yet become official policy. Black land rights were restricted to small reserves, pass laws controlled movements, and job color bars secured white economic privilege. When World War II erupted, these laws were firmly in place—though the war's demands would cause some temporary shifts in how strictly they were enforced.

---

7. World War II and Temporary Changes

Wartime Relaxations

As covered in earlier chapters, World War II (1939–1945) forced a slight easing of some segregation rules, especially in urban labor, because factories needed more workers. Certain color bars were informally bypassed to fill skilled or semi-skilled positions. Some Africans earned better wages during the war, and pass law enforcement was occasionally relaxed to ensure enough labor supply. Black workers experienced modest improvements in bargaining power, although these changes were not written into law.

Post-War Return to Strict Controls

Once the war ended, white legislators and officials reverted to stricter measures. They worried that Africans, having tasted higher wages and some freedoms, would demand permanent rights. In the late 1940s, calls to "tighten up" the pass system and re-segregate job categories grew louder. This sentiment contributed to the National Party's victory in 1948, as Afrikaner voters feared "dilution" of white privileges.

Thus, the war period's small liberalizations did not transform the underlying system. Instead, they underscored how quickly the government could shift policy to meet labor needs, then clamp down again when no longer required. The stage was set for a more comprehensive plan to enforce segregation.

8. Ideological Underpinnings of Segregation

"Separate Development" Concepts

Even before the term "apartheid" was used, many white officials and writers claimed that "separate development" was natural. They said

Africans, Coloureds, and Indians were "not ready" to live equally alongside whites. They cited "cultural differences" or "tribal traditions," ignoring how forcibly confining Africans to impoverished reserves had created many of the social problems they then blamed on Africans. Religious beliefs sometimes fed into this rationale, with some church leaders arguing that God intended distinct races to live apart.

Influence of Pseudo-Science

In the early 20th century, certain European and American theories of "racial superiority" also influenced South African policymakers. Though mostly discredited by mainstream science, ideas of "biological difference" were used to justify why Africans, they claimed, were better suited to menial labor. This pseudo-science emboldened leaders who wanted to maintain white "purity." The result was an environment where policies were rarely questioned on moral grounds, as the majority of the white electorate accepted these views or did not challenge them.

---

9. The Transition to Official Apartheid (1948)

The Rise of the National Party

As we explored in Chapters 17 and 18, the **National Party** capitalized on white fears and dissatisfaction with Jan Smuts's more moderate stance. In the 1948 election, **D.F. Malan** and his colleagues presented "apartheid" as a clear, systematic approach to existing segregation. They promised to unify white policy across the country, ensuring that Africans would remain separate—whether in rural "homelands" or controlled urban townships. The NP's win signaled the start of a new era in which these previously scattered segregation laws would be reorganized and intensified under one overarching policy.

A Legacy of Pre-Apartheid Laws

The new apartheid regime did not arise in a vacuum. It built on a foundation that had existed for decades:

- Pass laws restricting Black movements
- Land Acts confining African land ownership to reserves
- Urban Areas Acts segregating city housing
- Color bars reserving skilled jobs for whites
- Separate administrative systems for African affairs

All these elements laid the groundwork for the detailed, wide-ranging apartheid legislation of the 1950s. In many ways, the difference after 1948 was not the creation of brand-new ideas, but the coordination and expansion of existing practices into a far more rigorous system.

CHAPTER 20

THE THRESHOLD OF MODERN CONFLICT

Introduction

By the late 1940s, South Africa's long-standing segregation had entered a new phase. The **National Party**, victorious in the 1948 election, was determined to transform these scattered racial laws into a grand design called **apartheid**. Over the next few years, new legislation would classify every person by race, dictate who could live where, and ban almost all forms of racial mixing. This signaled the start of what we might call **modern conflict**—an era of intense struggle both within and outside the country.

Although this book stops short of detailing the full apartheid regime and later 20th-century events, we will close with a look at the immediate years after 1948—what we can call **"the threshold of modern conflict."** We will see how the new government formalized apartheid, how resistance began to shift toward more active defiance, and how the world started paying more attention to South Africa's internal affairs. By understanding these final steps in our historical journey, we gain insight into the roots of future confrontations, even though we will not travel beyond these historical times.

1. Malan's Early Apartheid Laws (1948–1950s)

Codifying Racial Categories

Shortly after taking office, **D.F. Malan** and his ministers introduced bills to classify the population by race. In 1950, Parliament passed the **Population Registration Act**, requiring all citizens to be registered as White, Coloured, Bantu (African), or Asian (Indian). Bureaucrats used arbitrary tests—skin color, hair texture, even "pencil tests" in hair—to label people. Families sometimes found themselves split across categories if a child's features differed from the parents.

This formal classification mattered because other laws—like the **Group Areas Act** (1950)—depended on it. If a family was classified "Coloured," they could be evicted from an area declared "White." If reclassified "White," a person might abandon relatives or fear a future reclassification. This system created deep stress and confusion, showing how the government's obsession with race could tear people's lives apart.

Group Areas Act

The **Group Areas Act** required towns and cities to be divided into separate racial zones. Mixed neighborhoods that had existed for generations—like **District Six** in Cape Town or **Sophiatown** in Johannesburg—were declared White areas. The government forced Black, Coloured, or Indian residents to move, often to remote, under-resourced townships. Businesses owned by non-Whites in these zones were also uprooted, sometimes at great financial loss.

In practice, the Act gave the state power to reshape entire cities in favor of White residents. Massive forced removals began in the early 1950s, continuing for decades. Although some English-speaking liberals criticized such harsh measures, the new NP government felt confident that a strong approach was needed to cement White security and Afrikaner ideals.

2. Enforcing Racial Separation in Daily Life

Pass Laws Strengthened

Existing pass laws were broadened. Now, all Africans had to carry **reference books** showing their employment status and personal details. If a police officer stopped a Black person without this reference book in proper order, they could face immediate arrest and deportation to a rural "homeland." Women, who previously were less strictly controlled by passes, also became subject to these laws under the new regulations. This sparked outrage among African women, some of whom began organizing protests that would eventually grow in the 1950s (famously leading to the 1956 Women's March, though that is beyond our current scope).

Banning Mixed Unions and Immorality

Building on earlier moves, the NP government passed the **Prohibition of Mixed Marriages Act (1949)** and the **Immorality Amendment Act (1950)**. These laws outlawed marriages and sexual relationships across racial lines. The police sometimes spied on suspected couples, intruding on private lives. Such laws aimed to prevent any blurring of racial categories, tying into the Population Registration Act. Many people saw these acts as deeply invasive, but those who supported apartheid argued that "racial purity" must be protected.

3. Resistance Shifts: The ANC and Others

Defiance Campaign Emerges

In reaction to these laws, **African National Congress (ANC)** leaders recognized they could not rely solely on petitions or deputations to government. Younger activists—like **Nelson Mandela**, **Walter Sisulu**, and **Oliver Tambo**—gained influence. Under their guidance, the ANC worked with the **South African Indian Congress** and other groups to plan **Defiance Campaigns** of non-violent protest. Although these major campaigns took place in the early 1950s, the planning began right after the National Party took power.

The idea was to break unjust laws deliberately—like going into "White Only" sections or burning passes—and accept arrest in large numbers. This approach drew on Gandhian satyagraha principles, but tailored to South African realities. The authorities responded with mass arrests, fines, and sometimes brutal police action. Even so, these campaigns signaled that oppression under apartheid would not go unchallenged.

Coloured and Indian Resistance

Coloured and Indian communities also faced forced removals and discriminatory laws. Indian South Africans, many living in Natal, were targeted by the Group Areas Act, which threatened to remove them from central Durban. Coloured people in the Cape lost their limited voting rights when the government passed laws placing them on a separate voters' roll. Parties like the **Anti-CAD** movement and the **South African Indian Congress** joined the ANC in forming a multi-racial front known as the **Congress Alliance**, though its major activities would peak mid-century.

While these alliances had only partial success early on, they laid groundwork for broader cooperation. Leaders realized that dividing the oppressed by race helped the government maintain control, so unity would be essential for any meaningful pushback.

---

4. International Criticism and Cold War Context

Growing International Disapproval

The post-war world, shaped by the **United Nations** and decolonization movements, was critical of racial discrimination. India, newly independent, raised complaints about the treatment of Indians in South Africa. Other Asian and African states also condemned apartheid policies. However, the **Western powers**, focused on the **Cold War** rivalry with the Soviet Union, tended to overlook South Africa's internal repression. They valued South Africa's strategic minerals (like gold and uranium) and did not want to alienate a potential anti-communist ally.

South Africa found itself increasingly isolated in bodies like the UN, yet it held onto alliances with Western nations for trade and strategic reasons. Prime Minister Malan and his successors insisted that outside criticism violated South Africa's sovereignty. They portrayed the conflict as a domestic matter, refusing UN or Commonwealth interventions.

The Logic of the Cold War

Because the global struggle between the **United States** and the **Soviet Union** dominated international politics, nations aligned with the West often gained a pass on human rights violations if they were seen as anti-communist. South Africa used this context to defend its policies, arguing that controlling Black populations was necessary to prevent communist infiltration. Though some Western politicians voiced moral objections, many accepted South Africa's stance due to Cold War calculations.

---

5. Economic Consequences of New Racial Rules

Business and Foreign Investment

The early apartheid laws did not stop foreign investment. Many British and American companies maintained profitable ventures in South Africa's mines, factories, and consumer markets. Cheap Black labor, enforced by pass laws and restricted unions, guaranteed high returns. While a few liberal businessmen expressed unease about overt racial policies, most were content so long as political stability favored profits.

At the same time, the government's emphasis on "Afrikaner upliftment" led to more white people, especially Afrikaners, getting managerial roles in state enterprises. Coloured and Indian entrepreneurs faced zoning regulations that forced them out of prime business areas, weakening their economic base. Africans remained locked in unskilled labor with minimal prospects for advancement.

Urban Reshaping

With the Group Areas Act in place, cities underwent major transformations. Johannesburg's mixed neighborhoods like **Sophiatown** were set for demolition; Cape Town's **District Six** also faced the bulldozers a bit later (in the 1960s, though planned earlier). Meanwhile, new all-white suburbs with good infrastructure expanded rapidly, funded by municipal budgets. This pattern not only shaped physical spaces but cemented the idea that certain amenities—paved roads, electricity, safe parks—were for whites only. Black townships received little public investment, fueling frustration and overcrowding.

6. Cultural Dimensions and Propaganda

Justifying Apartheid

The National Party used newspapers, radio broadcasts, and school textbooks to justify apartheid. They claimed separate development would "preserve cultural differences" and prevent racial conflicts. Some church groups—especially in the **Dutch Reformed Church**—supported these ideas, preaching that God had ordained distinct races to live apart. Though not all Afrikaner churches agreed, these teachings influenced many white congregations, easing moral doubts about the new laws.

Effects on Education

Afrikaner children learned in schools that apartheid was logical, while Black education was underfunded and often controlled by mission schools or tribal authorities. By the 1950s, the government would pass laws like the **Bantu Education Act** (1953), which set a separate, inferior curriculum for African students. But even before that, the seeds were sown: African youth had fewer schooling opportunities, ensuring a limited pool of skilled Black workers and reinforcing the labor hierarchy.

---

7. Opposition Within White Society

Liberal Whites

A small number of English-speaking liberals and church figures objected to strict racial policies. Groups like the **Black Sash**, founded by middle-class white women, peacefully protested issues such as the removal of Coloured voters from the electoral roll. Newspapers like the **Rand Daily Mail** published critical editorials. However, these voices remained a minority among white voters. They had little success in changing the NP's direction, given that the majority of white citizens saw apartheid as beneficial or necessary.

Academic Critiques

Some scholars at English-speaking universities—like **Wits** (University of the Witwatersrand) or **UCT** (University of Cape

Town)—produced studies showing that segregation policies harmed economic growth and social stability. They pointed out the moral and practical flaws of dividing society so rigidly. But the government dismissed these criticisms, occasionally labeling academics as "leftists" or "communists." In response, many intellectuals faced pressure or limited funding if they challenged official doctrine.

8. Growing Tensions Leading to Future Conflict

Mounting African Frustration

Black workers saw wages frozen by government regulations and job color bars firmly in place. Rapid urban growth continued, but housing remained inadequate. Pass raids, forced removals, and police brutality increased bitterness. Although major mass actions were still forming, small strikes and local protests flared. Younger activists, influenced by anti-colonial movements in other parts of Africa, felt more determined to resist, setting the stage for future direct confrontations.

Sharpening the Tools of Repression

The NP government passed new security measures, giving police broader powers to detain "subversive elements." As tension grew, authorities prepared for the possibility of larger uprisings. State agencies kept close watch on ANC leaders and allied movements, building files of personal data. In effect, the government was preparing an extensive repressive framework to handle any large-scale resistance that might arise.

9. The Symbolic Threshold of Modern Conflict

The 1950s Dawn

By the early 1950s, the foundations of **apartheid** were firmly set:

- **Population Registration**: Everyone was classified by race.
- **Group Areas**: Cities were mapped into racial zones, with forced removals looming.
- **Mixed Marriages Banned**: Racial lines in personal relationships were enforced by law.
- **Pass Laws**: African movement was strictly regulated.

Although the full scale of apartheid's brutality would emerge more clearly later (in the 1960s and beyond), the basic legal structure was established. Discrimination had been the norm before 1948, but now it was bigger, harsher, and more organized under the National Party's rule.

Outside Pressure and African Alliances

Neighboring African territories—still under colonial rule—watched carefully. African nationalism was rising across the continent, and soon, countries like **Ghana** (1957) would gain independence, encouraging anti-colonial movements elsewhere. South Africa's new government was out of step with this decolonizing trend, sowing seeds for future isolation. Meanwhile, the fledgling alliances among ANC, Indian Congress, and some Coloured groups indicated that internal unity was possible if they could overcome racial divisions. But the state's power to suppress dissent was immense.

---

10. Conclusion of Chapter 20

By the early 1950s, **South Africa** stood at the **threshold of modern conflict**—an era when the **apartheid system** took shape in law and daily life. The new National Party regime systematically enforced racial separation, building on the segregative measures of earlier decades. Urban areas were reshaped by forced removals, pass laws tightened, and labor color bars solidified white economic privilege. At the same time, the seeds of resistance were sown, with younger activists pushing for defiance campaigns and multi-racial alliances.

Although our account ends here—without diving into the full story of **apartheid** or the major events of the second half of the 20th century—these chapters show how a combination of historical segregation, wartime pressures, and Afrikaner nationalist victory in 1948 created a perfect storm. It locked South Africa into a path of deeper racial divisions. The struggles that lay ahead—mass protests, international condemnation, and eventual reform—were built on this backdrop of systematic oppression. By recognizing how deeply rooted these policies were, we grasp the scope of the conflicts that would later shake the country and the world's conscience.

Help Us Share Your Thoughts!

Dear reader,

Thank you for spending your time with this book. We hope it brought you enjoyment and a few new ideas to think about. If there was anything that didn't work for you, or if you have suggestions on how we can improve, please let us know at **kontakt@skriuwer.com**. Your feedback means a lot to us and helps us make our books even better.

If you enjoyed this book, we would be very grateful if you left a review on the site where you purchased it. Your review not only helps other readers find our books, but also encourages us to keep creating more stories and materials that you'll love.

By choosing Skriuwer, you're also supporting **Frisian**—a minority language mainly spoken in the northern Netherlands. Although **Frisian** has a rich history, the number of speakers is shrinking, and it's at risk of dying out. Your purchase helps fund resources to preserve and promote this language, such as educational programs and learning tools. If you'd like to learn more about Frisian or even start learning it yourself, please visit **www.learnfrisian.com**.

Thank you for being part of our community. We look forward to sharing more books with you in the future.

Warm regards,
The Skriuwer Team

www.ingramcontent.com/pod-product-compliance
Lightning Source LLC
LaVergne TN
LVHW012041070526
838202LV00056B/5554